ditch the ~~ditty~~.

Doing What Matters Instead of Doing It All

LINDSEY GODWIN, PHD
MOLLY MCGUIGAN, MBA
MIRIAM NOVOTNY, MPOD

ONION RIVER PRESS

Burlington, Vermont

Onion River Press
89 Church Street
Burlington, VT 05401
info@onionriverpress.com
www.onionriverpress.com

ISBN: 978-1-957184-78-4

Library of Congress Control Number: 2024919798

To the brilliant and courageous women on whose shoulders we stand—including the daughters, sisters, mothers, grandmothers, wives, friends, scholars, and thought leaders who have come before us and inspired us to dare to ditch the "shoulds" and embrace what truly matters— and to those still on the journey of finding their own path, this book is for you.

Contents

PREFACE
The Dawn of a Learning Journey

Once upon a time, in a convention center far, far away, two women led a multiday international event. After two years of organizing, thousands of hours of prep, and countless "I'll get right on that" emails, their big day finally arrived. Like conductors ensuring every note is perfect, they managed every detail of the four-day event. From facilitating the main stage for over 800 attendees from over 30 countries to keeping things smooth behind the scenes, they had their hands full. But apparently, they weren't full enough.

Imagine this scene:

Backstage with one of the keynote speakers, whom we'll call Mike, the two women were busy juggling several tasks. Suddenly, Mike turned to one of them, handed her his personal ditty bag—a small canvas bag for carrying personal odds and ends used by travelers—and said, "Here, hold this, it has my life in it." There were plenty of others who could have held the bag, or Mike could have simply set it down on a table provided for just such purposes. There was no reason for her to hold it, especially since she had 10 other things to do. But being the polite people-pleaser she was, she put down her other tasks and held his ditty bag until he retrieved it after his speech—without so much as a "thank you."

Though the woman didn't yet have the wherewithal to decline holding this particular ditty bag, she and her colleague did have the presence of mind to capture the moment. Clearly, they preferred documenting absurdity over avoiding it. See Exhibit A.

Later that evening, they shared the laughable picture with a third female colleague who dared to ask, "Why on earth did you hold his stupid ditty bag for him?" As the trio unpacked the incident together, a mix of emotions surfaced—annoyance, anger, and curiosity. They began sharing stories about other times they were handed something, literally or metaphorically, that they didn't want to deal with. They discussed what these things were and why they kept accepting them. After a few hours of laughter and tears, they realized that this little ditty bag story symbolized much more than it seemed.

SPOILER: The three women were us!

Molly was the one who got handed the literal ditty bag, while Lindsey snapped the infamous picture, and Miriam asked the question that sparked a learning journey we're still on today. Individually, we are three professional women who, by all traditional measures in today's world, would be considered successful. Earned advanced degrees? *Check!* Volunteered and contributed to our communities? *Check!* Led organizations? *Check!* Won professional awards? *Check!* Garnered respect from peers? *Check!* Have friends and family who support us? *Check!* Supported our families? *Check!* Remembered to water the plants? *Check!*

Yet, despite our achievements, we were struggling. Beneath our successes, we were saying "yes" to too many people and things, leaving us tired and burned out personally and professionally. This story is a perfect case in point. Molly, the leader of a huge project with many other demands on her time, stopped what she was doing to hold someone else's bag while he spoke for 20 minutes.

Exhibit A: Ditty Bag Ground Zero

The tale of "The Original Ditty Bag" became a turning point for us. It marked the moment we noticed dynamics in our lives in a new way. We recognized that—especially as women—we often do things we don't want or need to do. There are many reasons we do this: fear of repercussions, the desire to be nice, a need to seem perfect, or simply discomfort with saying "no." Mike handing his ditty bag to Molly in the convention center all those years ago has since turned into a powerful metaphor for us. We coined the term "Ditty" to describe anything we agree to out of politeness, obligation, or fear of upsetting someone, even when we don't want or need to do it.

With a clear word for these moments, we could finally start to notice when we say "yes" to things we don't want or need to do. Ditties can take many forms. From agreeing to extra projects at work, to soothing a friend's drama, to being the go-to person for everyone's emotional support, to taking on extra household duties, to constantly saying "yes" to social invitations you don't really want to attend, Ditties come in all shapes and sizes. A Ditty can even be the stories we hold about ourselves that do not serve us—not being good enough, pretty enough, or capable enough—that keep us trapped in cycles of self-doubt and unnecessary obligations.

When we dared to look at our calendars through this new lens, we discovered Ditties lurking in every corner of our lives. It hit us—we were constantly trying to do it all and make everyone happy, leaving us buried in an avalanche of Ditties. No wonder we felt so tired and overwhelmed! When we started talking about Ditties with other women in our lives, we quickly learned that everyone we knew had examples of Ditties they had picked up, too. Stories bubbled up, like:

- Hosting a family gathering, knowing it meant days of unwanted cleaning, cooking, and managing quirky relatives.

- Taking on a coworker's task despite not having extra time because they asked politely while flashing a pretty-please-puppy-dog look.

- Saying "yes" to a social event when we'd prefer to be at home in pajamas with a good book.

- Baking cupcakes for a fundraiser even when feeling there's barely time to cook dinner.

- Agreeing to take minutes at a meeting *again* even when others could do it.

Curiosity struck us about why women in particular take on Ditties. To better understand this tendency, we dove into the research on gender dynamics and gendered socialization.*

This exploration led us to topics such as:

- *Office Housework*[1]

- *The Confidence Chasm*[2]

- *Imposter Syndrome*[3]

- *Boundaries*[4]

- *People Pleasing*[5]

- *Apologizing*[6]

- *Women's Unpaid Labor*[7]

- *Gendered Self-Concepts*[8]

While anyone can end up with Ditties, research shows that women are often socialized to be nice, helpful, and accommodating, frequently at the expense of their own needs.[9] Such social conditioning leads many women to take on unwanted burdens to avoid conflict or disappointment much more than their male counterparts

Understanding why we as women often pick up Ditties was just our first step. Once we became more aware of the reasons behind our tendency to say "yes" to things we don't want nor need to do, our next challenge was figuring out how to break that habit. We

*In exploring the dynamics that impact women, we wholeheartedly acknowledge and respect the diverse spectrum of sex and gender identities. While our focus in this book centers on the experiences of cisgender women, we honor and recognize the unique journeys of individuals across the gender spectrum. Although many of the dynamics described throughout our work apply to anyone who identifies as a woman, we understand that the stories and research highlighted herein do not fully capture the complex experiences of transgender or nonbinary women, which deserve their own unique exploration beyond the scope of this book.

wanted to shed these unwanted burdens and stop picking them up altogether. This led us to the idea of "Ditching Ditties" which means letting go of unnecessary and unwanted obligations and tasks, including the invisible labor often imposed on women.[10]

We realized that Ditty Ditching is essential for us as women because it allows us to reclaim our time, energy, and autonomy. Letting go of these unwanted obligations reduces stress, improves well-being, and helps us live more authentically. Recognizing the importance of Ditching Ditties, we became curious about the Ditties other women pick up and how they have learned to Ditch them.

We conducted interviews with women in our lives to gather qualitative data on their experiences with both Ditties and Ditching. Initially, we interviewed women of different ages and backgrounds, asking them questions such as:

- When have you picked up Ditties and why?

- What are the different ways Ditties are delivered to you?

- When have you passed Ditties on to others?

- How have you Ditched Ditties you no longer want to carry?

- How do you determine what is and isn't a Ditty in your life?

Through these conversations, we were able to begin identifying common patterns and insights into the motivations and strategies behind successfully avoiding and Ditching Ditties. Using these findings, we expanded our exploration, and we continued having dialogues with other women and testing our ideas and practices with them. To date, we've gathered stories from over 150 women, spanning different ages, races, nationalities, and sexual orientations. Their diverse perspectives and experiences provide a rich and varied collection of insights.

Armed with a blend of insights and stories from these women, as well as data and research on gender dynamics, we began writing this book and creating workshops for women to explore intentional decision-making in their lives. We had the date, place, and participants for our first in-person workshop all set…then a global pandemic sent us all home for over a year.

As we navigated the sudden upheaval of working from home, supporting our children through virtual schooling, and facing each day anew, our energy was zapped. We won't lie—we lost our mojo for a while and wondered, "Given all that's happening in the world, who's going to want to talk about Ditching Ditties?"

But amid our pandemic-impacted lives, headlines started popping up such as:

- *Why Women Are Leaving the Workforce After the Pandemic— And How to Win Them Back*[11]

- *Some Gender Disparities Widened in the U.S. Workforce During the Pandemic*[12]

- *Return-to-Office Mandates Are a Disaster for Working Mothers*[13]

Suddenly, it seemed that there was a crescendo of conversations happening about the pandemic-exacerbated inequalities women face in both the workplace and home space. And somewhere in between reading these headlines and continuing to do our own regular Ditty-Ditching work together on Zoom each week, something happened…we got our mojo back!

Re-energized by the realization that conversations on Ditching Ditties are more important than ever, we recognized that the unique challenges women face have not changed. We are still navigating return-to-work decisions, ongoing disparities in family responsibilities, and a culture that expects us to always smile and be helpful.

With renewed commitment, we rolled up our sleeves and dove back into our Ditty-Ditching work. Drawing upon our combined six decades of expertise in organizational change, education, and personal development (check out our bios in the appendix), we dedicated ourselves to creating spaces that help women build awareness and skills around their everyday choices. Our goal is to empower women to intentionally decide what to Ditch and what to keep.

The more women we talked to, the more we realized the importance of addressing our Ditty challenges with humor, compassion, and depth. We didn't want to create another conversation where women felt inadequate or like they weren't "doing it right." Instead, we aim to create spaces where we can collectively reflect on our shared experiences as women, laugh at the absurdities we face, and provide practical tools and tips to "shed the shoulds" we often carry. Our goal will always be to help women love themselves along their Ditty-Ditching journey.

Today, we think of ourselves as *The Ditty-Ditching Divas*, lovingly irreverent rebels who defy outdated gender expectations with humor and healthy disregard for norms. *Ditch the Ditty* is our playful rebellion, inviting women to be norm-shakers and joy-makers in their lives. In the following pages, we've crafted a Ditty-Ditching universe in which we hope you'll be able to see yourself. While we've learned a lot about Ditching pesky Ditties, every conversation we have with other women brings new insights on how to Ditch unwanted Ditties and bring more delight into our lives.

We also recognize that research on women and gender dynamics is constantly evolving, reshaping our understanding of societal norms and roles. For example, the COVID pandemic highlighted existing inequalities and prompted a reevaluation of traditional gender roles. Daily politics surrounding women's rights, bodies, and access to equal pay add new chapters to this ongoing story. At the same time, social media is helping women share information—and their lived experiences— in ways they haven't been able to in the past. This book reflects our current insights, acknowledging that we are writing in a specific moment in an ever-changing world. While it's easy to feel overwhelmed by these shifts, we're inspired by Maya Angelou's wisdom: "Do the best you can until you know better. Then, when you know better, do better."[14] We recognize that as new research and realities emerge, we may need to reconsider what we "know," including the ideas in this book.

While our Ditty-Ditching work has created ripples beyond our wildest dreams, it remains deeply personal to us. We'll never forget those three women who were handed that original Ditty and their journey since. The three of us continue to support each other with the insights and tools in this book. Though we sometimes fall off the Ditty-Ditching wagon, we always help each other Ditch unwanted Ditties and embrace life's delights. This is the journey we hope you'll go on as well—creating support systems for yourself as you begin to recognize and release the Ditties in your own life.

If we've learned anything, it's that perhaps the biggest Ditty to Ditch is the illusion of perfection. So, is this book perfect? No. But that won't stop us from embracing our perfectly imperfect selves and sharing our work. We invite you to join us on this journey of discovery, insight, impact and—most importantly—laughter. This book is more than just a read; it's an invitation to join our evolving Ditty-Ditching community. Connect with us and other Ditty-Ditching Divas at www.ditchtheditty.com.

Now, are you ready? Let's Ditch some Ditties together so we can carry less—less stress…less anxiety…less pressure…less perfectionism…less of the internalized dynamics that no longer serve us—and live more delightfully!

PART 1
What Are Ditties & Why Ditch Them?

Sometimes the word is out of our mouths before we even realize it. Just three little letters that individually seem so harmless but collectively can wreak so much havoc in our lives. What are these precarious—possibly perilous—letters?

Y–E–S

"Yes...I will help you with that project."

"Yes...I will take notes at the meeting."

"Yes...I will organize the family holiday gathering."

"Yes...I will volunteer to lead that group."

"Yes...I will bring gluten-free, sugar-free, egg-free cupcakes to the bake sale."

"Yes...I will _____." [Fill in the blank with something you really did NOT want to do but said "yes" to anyway.]

You've done it before. You've probably already done it 10 times today.

Don't worry, we've done it too.

We've all said "yes" to requests when our brains and hearts were internally whispering—or perhaps not-so-silently yelling—"No, no, please no!" We've all had those moments where we're handed something by someone else...a task, a project, a responsibility, a social expectation of how to behave, you name it...that we didn't *really* want to do, nor did we *really* have to do it, but we did it anyway.

These "I-should-have-said-no" moments are DITTIES—those things we agree to even though we don't really want to or need to.

Why do we call them Ditties?

A "ditty bag" traditionally refers to a small canvas bag for carrying personal odds and ends. Historically, they were used by sailors to carry their thread and needles while out at sea. Fun fact: these little bags were also referred to as a "housewife" once upon a time, so let that etymology sink in for a moment![15] Today, ditty bags are typically thought of as small travel bags for carrying everyday items.

Remember, as our original ditty bag story in the Preface illustrates, when someone hands you their ditty bag, it's filled with *their* stuff, not yours. Let's restate that: **It is not YOUR stuff.**

We define a Ditty as:

Ditty

/ˈdidē/ *noun*
1. an unnecessary task that you don't want to do
2. a request that doesn't match your values or priorities
3. an ingrained socialized habit that isn't helpful to you

Individually, Ditties seem small and harmless. Holding one or two for someone else usually isn't stressful, depending on how "heavy" the metaphorical items are. As Ditties pile up, however, we feel worn down at best, or angry and resentful at worst. Tending to Ditties takes time and energy away from other things, things that we actually **want** to be doing, things that align with what's essential to us, or dare we say, things that bring us joy.

Both men[*] and women can pick up Ditties, but women seem to collect them like they're going out of style. Why do we, as women, so often accept these devilish little Ditties? Thanks to society's pressure for women to be accommodating and polite,[16] we often feel obligated to shoulder everyone's extra baggage, even when it weighs us down. "Women have this invisible burden of caretaking that's often ignored or devalued," says Dr. Nicole Johnson, assistant professor of counseling psychology.[17] This pressure results in us prioritizing others over ourselves, leading to habitual Ditty acceptance and ultimately causing chronic stress, burnout, and a loss of self-autonomy.[18] Reflecting on the American Psychological Association's guidelines,[19] which show higher mental health risks for women, Dr. Johnson states, "These rates differ not because of being a woman, but because of the societal consequences of being a woman."[20]

As a woman, we're sure that you've felt the pressure to be polite, to avoid the appearance of rudeness, and not to disappoint others, leading you to agree to things you didn't want to do. Heaven forbid you offend someone, let anyone down, or shirk what you mistakenly believe is your responsibility! There are 101 reasons—all of which seem perfectly rational at the time—that Ditties sneak into our lives.

The three of us juggle professional, social, and family roles—in a world with specific expectations of women for each. As such, we are constantly feeling the tug of Ditties in our lives, probably just as you are. That's why we wrote this book. We created it for ourselves and for you—to help us all navigate and conquer the

---

*It's important to recognize that gender socialization affects men too. For example, the current discussions around toxic masculinity are fascinating and important, but that's a topic worthy of another book.

challenges of Ditties and focus on what truly matters in our lives. So, whether you're clocking in at an office, dealing with the pressures of school, running the show at home, or just trying to manage your life, this book is for you. It's for every woman[†] who's been trying to be everything to everyone while juggling the pressure to be the perfect, polite, helpful person that others expect her to be. Our goal is to share the experiences, insights, and strategies we've developed over the past six years to help you reclaim your time and energy. This book is your irreverent guide to Ditching Ditties and focusing on what truly matters.

To begin, we have some good news and bad news for you.

The good news: We all pick up Ditties.

The bad news: We all pick up Ditties.

On one hand, you are in good company with us and the millions of other women who have picked up, and continue to pick up, Ditties. It's nothing to be ashamed of. In fact, it's a great conversation starter with friends and family. For example, when there's a lull when chatting with a colleague, you could say, "I just got a crazy Ditty handed to me from the marketing department, how was your day?" Or when the turkey coma sets in after Thanksgiving dinner, wake everyone up by asking about the new Ditties Granny assigned during the meal prep. Did you really need to pre-wash the turkey three times to ensure she'd eat it?

Like trading war stories and showing each other your battle scars, we guarantee that other women in your life will have their own Ditty stories to share.

On the other hand, we're swimming in a social culture that expects women to pick up Ditties and do so with a smile. We've all been handed countless Ditties and just sucked them up and dealt with them, smiling or not. Given the sheer volume of Ditties we've each dealt with in our lives, we've normalized holding Ditties as just part of life. We accept Ditties without thinking—and often

---

†As we shared in the preface, although we acknowledge the diverse spectrum of sex and gender identities, this book focuses on cisgender women's experiences. While we hope anyone who identifies as a woman finds valuable insights here, we believe the unique experiences of transgender and nonbinary women deserve their own exploration beyond this book's scope.

without even realizing it. Just like in blackjack, we often agree to just "one more," thinking we can manage it, until we inevitably hit our limit and go bust.

Don't worry. We have one more piece of good news:

With every Ditty, you have a choice.

That's right. While it may not always feel like it, we have a choice when it comes to picking up and holding a Ditty. This isn't to say that our choices are without consequences. But the truth is, we always have a choice in whether we say that little three-letter word: Y-E-S, or if we decide to say those two other magical letters: N-O.

We realize that "no" sometimes feels more like a four-letter word than a two-letter one. Given the dynamics that are evoked by this simple little declaration, we'll further explore a variety of ways you can scale your "no" later in the book. For the moment, we simply invite you to internalize the notion of *choice*.

Like Keanu Reeves' character, Neo, in *The Matrix* choosing between the blue and red pill, this is perhaps your chance to wake up to the fact that you also have a choice.[21] You can choose to see the Ditties in your own life and be more intentional in what you do or don't accept from others in the future so that you have more time and energy for those things that are essential to you. Or you can keep indiscriminately accepting Ditties and continue to wonder why you feel overwhelmed and undervalued. No judgment— we've been there! We just want you to realize you're choosing to accept Ditties and to make that choice intentionally.

But what if you decided to start Ditching those Ditties instead?

And just what does it mean to Ditch something? We define it as:

Ditch

/' diCH/ *verb*
1. to get rid of or give up something
2. to unaccept something you never wanted in the first place

Ditching is crucial for reclaiming your time and energy, reducing stress, and focusing on what truly matters. By saying "no" to unnecessary obligations and outdated gender norms, you can prioritize your needs and regain control of your life. We want you to recognize this potential within yourself because this shift in perspective is empowering. The truth is, we see ourselves more like Glinda the Good Witch from *The Wizard of Oz*[22] than Morpheus from *The Matrix*.[23] We're simply here to remind you that "You've always had the power [to Ditch Ditties], my dear, you just had to learn it for yourself."[24]

To kickstart your own Ditching adventures, we're introducing our first "Bite-Size Challenge." These micro-practices are sprinkled throughout the book, offering manageable tasks to try in your own life. Designed to be small and satisfying—without inviting you to bite off more than you can chew—they will give you a taste of accomplishment and build your appetite for bigger Ditching successes.

A Bite-Size Challenge

Awareness is one of our best friends when it comes to Ditching Ditties. Reflect on a time when you accepted a Ditty and a time you didn't. What stands out between those two stories? What was the impact of saying "yes" and "no" in those situations? What can you learn from these experiences?

As you start experimenting with Ditching Ditties to reclaim your time and energy, it's critical that we also recognize the role of privilege in this process.

The Privilege to Ditch

We feel it's very important to acknowledge that the ability to say "no" to Ditties can be a position of privilege. Not everyone has the luxury to refuse tasks without facing potential negative consequences, such as strained relationships, job loss, social exclusion, or feeling unsafe. Saying "no" may be easier for some due to their socio-economic status, job security, or support network. Therefore, it's crucial to weigh the potential impacts and consequences before declining a commitment.

Stay mindful of your unique situation and find ways to minimize any fallout—like being honest, setting boundaries slowly, or leaning on trusted friends for support. Tackle Ditching with sensitivity to yourself and those around you. And while we offer many insights here about when and how to Ditch an unwanted ask or obligation, remember: **You** are the one who best knows when and how to Ditch in your own life!

The 4-Ds of Decision-Making: Ditties, Deeds, Duties, & Delights

Let's take a closer look to understand what Ditties are and aren't. To better identify Ditties, we first need to look at the many tasks, requests, and expectations that come our way—or are sometimes dumped on our doorstep like an unwanted, smelly surprise, with the giver conveniently disappearing. The first step in determining if something is, or isn't, a Ditty is to ask yourself:

"Is this something I want to do?"

Don't let this question fool you. On the surface, this seems like such an easy one to answer. Because of course, we're always *oh so clear* on what we want and don't want, right? But if you're anything like us, you might find this to be one of the most challenging questions you'll ever ask yourself.

As women, we've internalized so many ideas from others about what we *should* want that it's easy to confuse "ought tos" with "wants." The narratives from our childhood, family, friends, work, and society echo in our heads, acting like a jury every time we make a decision. Here are a few stories that have taken up residence in our minds—see if they sound familiar to you.

- My parents taught me that good girls help others, so being a good person means I must want to help whenever someone asks.

- School taught me that playing nice with others gets rewarded, so to be accepted, I must smile and collaborate on projects when invited.

- Work taught me that getting ahead means continually showing my value, so to be successful, I should agree to take on responsibilities when others ask.

With all the noise we've collected in our heads from others, it's perhaps no wonder that clarifying what we *really* want versus what we think we *should* want is no easy feat. In Part 2, we'll explore further how to unpack those voices in our heads and where they came from, helping us better separate our "ought tos" from our true "wants." For now, we recognize the challenge of truly knowing what you want and the tendency to answer hastily. So, after asking yourself, "*Is this something I want to do?*" add this follow-up question:

"Is this something I REALLY want to do?"

See what we did there? We added one little but mighty word: "really." Who knew six letters strung together could be so powerful? We use the word "really" to invite you to stop and reflect on your answer. Yep, we need a built-in pause in our decision-making to help ensure we're not running on autopilot, letting those voices in our head make decisions for us.

As we reflected on the many times we took on unwanted Ditties, we realized that we often accepted them because we didn't pause to reflect on the true power of choice we had in the decision. Instead, we were swept up by a heightened sense of responsibility, fear of letting someone down, or angst about saying "no." Let's illustrate with one of our many personal "oh-that-was-totally-a-Ditty-I-should-have-Ditched" examples.

The Ditty Diaries: Molly's Story

I was asked to take over as the president of a local volunteer board, a role I neither wanted nor needed. As an engaged person in my community, I felt like I should step up. Thoughts of obligation swirled in my mind—shouldn't I contribute more? Shouldn't I use my skills to help out? If I didn't step up, what would happen if no one else did either? When the moment to respond came, the weight of these perceived responsibilities overshadowed my sense of choice. Without much reflection, I found myself blurting out an unenthusiastic "yes," even though my head and heart were saying, "You don't need to do this...and you don't really want to do this."

Just because the request asked of Molly wasn't presented with flashing red lights declaring it a Ditty didn't mean choice was absent. Choice is often much quieter than the other voices in our head—obligation, responsibility, guilt, fear—clamoring for our attention when making a decision. In most cases, when we're maneuvering through those critical decision moments and we're faced with whether we should say "yes" or "no" to something, we don't take the time to pause and give choice a moment to raise its head in the sea of other things swimming around in our mind. Yet, one of the best lessons we've discovered in our own Ditty-Ditching journey is:

There is power in the pause.

A pause can help create space to recognize that, more often than not, a choice exists when we are being asked to do something. A pause can help us more clearly notice Ditties.

In responding to the presidency request, Molly never paused to evaluate if she wanted the role. She didn't consider the attention it would take from other things she valued. She also didn't identify what else she would need to say "no" to in order to manage this "yes."

> **NEWSFLASH:** There are only 24 hours in a day, no matter how many "yeses" we try to cram in. Every "yes" is like a little time thief, swiping moments from something else, while every "no" is like a superhero, rescuing time for other commitments and future opportunities—or simply time for ourselves.

As a result of not pausing to reflect on the time trade-off, Molly agreed to the presidency role. She quickly realized, however, that it was a Ditty filled with other people's stuff, draining her time and energy from the things she truly wanted to do.

A Bite-Size Challenge

What if you paused for 24 hours the next time you were asked to take on a new task before deciding? Try it! Then, reflect on:

→ What did you notice...about yourself...about the situation...about your options?

→ What stories did you tell yourself?

→ How did taking a pause give you space to determine if you wanted to do it?

So, we invite you to pause and consider whether the requests made of you are things you *really* want to do. If your answer is "YES!" then congratulations! Something you genuinely want to do isn't a Ditty; it's what we call a Delight—something that brings you joy. Go forth and enjoy doing it. Like Ditties, Delights can come in all shapes and sizes. They might be as simple as spending time with loved ones, or achieving a professional goal, or pursuing a favorite hobby, or traveling somewhere new, or even just enjoying a relaxing self-care day. Delights appear in our personal and professional lives, and they are our greatest wish for you! After all, one of the biggest motivations for Ditching Ditties is to have more time for Delights in our life. We define them as:

Delight

/dih-LITE/ *noun*
1. a task or action you want to do
2. a commitment that brings you joy and pleasure in completing it

However, if your answer feels like a "maybe," then it's really a "no," because "maybes" are just "nos" in disguise. When you realize this isn't something you *really* want to do, you have another question to ask yourself:

"Is it required?"

If your answer to this question is "yes," then guess what—we're going to throw one more "really" at you. Yep, here's another invitation to **pause** and ask yourself:

"Is it REALLY required?"

Once again, we often jump too quickly into assuming that something is required just because it's being asked of us. Taking another moment to pause and decipher if the task is indeed something that's *actually* your responsibility is important before you commit to taking it on.

But let's assume it's really required of you. After all, there are things that we need to do as part of our accepted roles and responsibilities. From commitments we've made in our work life, to our home life, or even to ourselves, there are things we do to maintain a productive life. For example, grocery shopping may top your "ugh-not-this-again!" list. But if you want to have food in your fridge without becoming a homesteader, you head to the grocery store and fill your cart up. Even if every trip down the same aisles feels like you're Bill Murray in *Groundhog Day*,[25] it's a necessary activity to have food to eat. Thus, grocery shopping is a required task.

If something is truly required of you, even if you're not necessarily jumping up and down to do it, we define it as a Duty.

Duty

/' dၴŏdē/ *noun*
1. a necessary responsibility or obligation
2. a task or action you need to do because of other desires or commitments

Now, that said, we do want to dive deeper into the idea of Duties, because they're complicated little things that can easily trip us up. And it's so easy to fall into the trap of thinking that everything we don't like is automatically a Ditty. Let's look at another real-life example.

The Ditty Diaries: Lindsey's Story

My sister, Natalie, texted me a picture of her two kiddos during their nightly bath time regimen. One is happily splashing while the other, with a curious and proud expression, holds a piece of poop in her hand she just contributed to the tub. The first kid grins blissfully, unaware, while the second proudly examines her discovery. Water droplets and bubbles add to the chaotic, comical scene. The picture was accompanied by a text from Natalie:

> Bath time fail. That's a shit. To my credit, I didn't realize it while I was snapping pictures, but did immediately after this.

Moments later, a second text followed:

> I had to bare hand it to get it out. It's not pretty, but very funny.

After I stopped snort-laughing at this hilariously vivid scene my sister had shared, I of course immediately told Miriam and Molly about it. The three of us reflected on how our family roles are a wonderful example of the fact that we often do things we don't like but still need to do.

This tale led us to the revelation:

Just because it's sh*tty, doesn't make it a Ditty.

Sometimes, we must do things in life that are literally sh*tty. As Natalie's hilarious text illustrated, cleaning up puke, pee, and other bodily functions and fluids is all in a day's work of having kids. Cleaning up the bathtub mess was not something Natalie really wanted to do, but she did it because she loves her kiddos—and wanted to use the tub again! She realized that sometimes these unpleasantries are simply part of the duties of being a parent.

But you don't have to be a parent to experience this.

Caretaking roles can come in all shapes and sizes and may often involve tasks we don't want to do but we take on out of love and responsibility. For example, those of us who are pet owners often face unpleasant tasks, such as cleaning litter boxes or picking up after walks—all for the sake of our furry friends. Those of us who care for aging parents or relatives perform tasks like bathing or feeding, driven by love and duty. If you're in this particular caretaking role, you're not alone. Women comprise nearly 60% of unpaid caregivers and over 80% of paid in-home caregivers for seniors.[26]

Beyond their personal lives, women often find themselves in professional caregiving roles as well. For instance, 77% of K-12 teachers are women, who frequently spend additional hours grading papers or handling classroom conflicts to aid their students' development.[27] Healthcare providers frequently handle unpleasant tasks like cleaning wounds or dealing with difficult patients to ensure their well-being. And guess who comprises the majority of registered nurses who are often performing these tasks? Yep, over 87% are women[28] (but male nurses, by the way, get paid $14,000 more on average than their female counterparts[29]).

Regardless of your job and relationships, some tasks at home, with friends, family, or at work will be unpleasant—but that doesn't automatically make them Ditties. There are necessary parts of our roles that we may not like, and yes, they can be pretty sh*tty. At home, unclogging a drain is a necessary but unpleasant job. Doing laundry might make you feel like you're constantly in a spin cycle, but having clean clothes is something that keeps you from smelling ripe. Going to the dentist might feel like nails on a chalkboard to you, but maintaining healthy teeth is something you want. As a friend, helping someone pack and move is tedious and exhausting, but we do it to support them.

If you have a job, consider the things you do at work that you hate but you do them because they're part of your job description. Maybe you detest conducting performance reviews for the people you supervise, but you do it because it's a requirement of the job. Perhaps email is the bane of your existence, or filing those expense reports feels like you're being probed by aliens, or _____ [fill in the blank with whatever crappy task you'd rather not do at work]. Yet, these are pieces and parts of the role you accepted when you agreed to do a particular job.

Because they are necessary tasks, we don't Ditch Duties. Instead, we invite you to do them your own unique way. By adding a personal touch and making them enjoyable, you can transform even the most mundane Duty into something less icky and perhaps even a bit delightful!

A Bite-Size Challenge

If you find yourself stuck with a sh*tty Duty, we invite you to **do it your way**, by bringing your own special flavor of fun to it!

Don't like emailing?

→ Create a fun signature line that's attached to every email you send out, like a little ray of light in an otherwise dark sky. For example: *P.S. Life's a whirlwind, and I'm loving every minute of it. Your email is part of the fun and will be responded to as soon as possible!*

Don't like doing laundry for what feels like the 4,531st time?

→ Use the time as an excuse to catch another two (or 10) episodes of that Netflix show you've been binging.

Don't like cleaning poop out of the bathtub from a kid or pet?

→ Pop on some tunes and rock out while you do it (we suggest Snoop Dogg's *Drop It Like It's Hot* for such an occasion).

Don't like sitting in that two-hour online meeting listening to information that could have been shared in a three-sentence email?

→ Make a bingo card of phrases you know you'll hear during the meeting and see how long it takes you to "win!" For example:

Can you hear me?	I can't share my screen.	Quick question...
I have a hard stop.	FREE SPACE	Just to piggyback on that...
Sorry, I was on mute.	Let's take this offline.	Can you repeat that?

We've used each of these "do-it-your-way" tricks for our own Duties. And, no matter the task, you can bring your unique personality to it and have fun! However, if you find that the *majority* of your Duties in a particular role feel like a steaming pile of manure, it might be time to re-examine your commitment to that role.

While we recognize that we can't just walk away from roles like caretaking of family members, there are other roles that we do have the ability to change. And remember that one person's mess is another's masterpiece. There are people who love doing what you find unpleasant (yes, some people love filing expense reports!). And we promise you that there's a wide world out there with opportunities that involve things you actually want to be doing…but it may take courage to go find them.

> **Pop quiz:** What's the litmus test for distinguishing a Ditty from a Duty? (It's an open book test, so feel free to scan previous pages for the answer.)

> **Answer:** With every Ditty, you have a **CHOICE.**

Although sometimes it's not immediately clear, a Duty is truly required of us, whereas a Ditty is optional and is really our choice.

We know that you're likely thinking: "Great, I need to pause and give myself time to think before saying 'yes,' but how else can I spot a Ditty?" We've introduced you to the notion of Delights and clarified Duties from Ditties, but there's one more decision-point we need to explore.

Let's say you've decided that you don't really want to do something **AND** it's not really required of you. Where does that leave you? It would be easy to say that it's wise to just say "no" to whatever this request is; however, life is more complicated than that. Occasionally, we take on unnecessary and unwanted obligations because they help us in other areas. Saying "yes" to such tasks can be a strategic move toward achieving larger goals. For example:

- Sitting through a dull training session to gain an extra professional certificate that will look great on your resume.

- Helping a family member move (again!) knowing they'll return the favor when your moving day comes in six months.

- Taking on a tedious extra project at work to show your dedication and inch closer to that coveted promotion.

- Helping a friend ace a subject you're a whiz at so they'll return the favor when you need a study buddy for something you struggle with.

- Volunteering at a community event you're not into to meet interesting people and expand your network.

As such, even if the answer to the question "Is it really required?" is "no," we invite you to ask yourself:

"Does it give me an opportunity?"

According to Merriam-Webster,[30] an "opportunity" is:

1. *a favorable juncture of circumstances*
2. *a good chance for advancement or progress*

Occasionally, we encounter opportunities to do unwanted and unnecessary tasks that pave the way for something else we truly desire. This might be a chance to meet someone, impress others, gain favor, build a quid pro quo, develop a skill, or do anything else that benefits us now or in the future. Consider the following two examples.

The Ditty Diaries: Lindsey's Story

A few years ago, I was invited at the last minute to facilitate a two-day strategic retreat for a group of interesting folks. This invitation came while I was on vacation, meaning I'd have to hop on a plane the next day and miss out on two days of family beach time. The role wasn't particularly wanted or required as it was outside my job scope—

and was going to interrupt my precious sand-in-the-toes moments. Plus, it was a pro-bono gig with only expenses covered, so money wasn't even a motivating factor. I could have easily said "no" and continued enjoying my sandy paradise without any severe consequences aside from the guilt of turning down my colleague's request. But while this request could have easily been Ditched as an unwanted Ditty, it dangled a unique opportunity that was hard to resist. It was a chance to rub elbows and build connections with some fascinating, high-profile individuals in my field. Plus, it was a golden opportunity to practice leading a small group's strategic planning process—a skill I was itching to add to my professional tool kit. In the end, I said "yes," hopped on a plane, facilitated for two days, and then rushed back to rejoin my family and stick my toes back in the sand.

The Ditty Diaries: Ally's Story[*]

I've never been a fan of book clubs and have always preferred to read alone, curled up in my favorite chair with a cup of tea. But when I was asked to join a local book club that some well-connected women in my community were part of, I decided to give it a shot. It seemed like a great opportunity to meet new people and expand my network. I committed to attending the meetings for a few months to see how it would go. At first, it felt a bit awkward, but soon enough, I found myself enjoying the opportunity to connect with some really fun women. Even though it wasn't something I initially wanted to do, it turned out to be a rewarding experience. Networking with them has opened up other opportunities for me in the community, leading to exciting collaborations and new friendships.

So, what were these asks that Lindsey and Ally faced? They weren't immediate Delights, nor were they exactly Ditties or Duties. We've come to refer to these as "Deeds"—things we don't really want to

---

*We're using pseudonyms for stories that we're sharing that aren't our own.

do and aren't required to, but that present us with an opportunity. They're tasks we undertake with intentionality and for a clearly defined amount of time.

Deed

/dēd/ *noun*
1. an unnecessary task or action you don't want to do but take on because it offers other opportunities
2. a clearly defined task done intentionally for a set amount of time

Deeds are things we say "yes" to, but it's important to be cautious. We advise that you do them carefully. Be intentional about *why* you're doing the Deed by explicitly identifying the opportunity it offers. Set clear boundaries, including the length of time you'll commit to the Deed. Additionally, ask yourself:

"Does it align with my values?"

If the answer to this question is "no," then no matter how golden the opportunity, it's not for you. No Deed is worth compromising your values or who you are as a person. And if you're not fully clear on your values, don't worry. We have an entire section in Part 4 to help you explore them further.

Let's consider Lindsey's story above. If she had been invited to facilitate a strategic retreat for the executives of a tobacco company, it wouldn't have aligned with her personal values of working only with organizations that promote health and well-being. However, since the group she facilitated was all about exploring how businesses could become more socially responsible, it matched Lindsey's values perfectly.

Last, but not least, even if an ask presents an opportunity *and* aligns with your values, you still have one more tire to kick before you sign your name on the dotted line:

"Does it align with my priorities?"

Sure, something may offer you an opportunity and align with your values, but does it also fit with your current priorities? Remember that newsflash we shared with you earlier? We're serious—there really are only 24 hours in a day. So, before you agree to any Deed, **PAUSE** and look at your entire game board. What other pieces are you currently trying to move forward? Considering everything else you're juggling, does this Deed help you in a way that's meaningful and important? Sam's story is a great concrete example of this.

The Ditty Diaries: Sam's Story

After graduating from college, I was offered an amazing internship opportunity with a prestigious company. The role promised to be a good addition to my resume, even though I already had a great job lined up for the fall. However, the internship required me to move to a different city for the summer. I had just spent the past four years buried in textbooks and projects, and I had made plans to spend the summer with my friends, celebrating our graduation and creating memories before we all went our separate ways. After much consideration, I decided to turn down the internship. While it was a fantastic opportunity, it didn't align with my current priorities. I wanted to cherish that special time with my friends and enjoy the freedom of summer. I imagined that if I had taken that internship instead of spending the summer with my friends—and then heard all the fun stories they were sharing—I would have likely felt resentful of the internship, despite it being a good opportunity. It was a difficult decision, but one that felt right for me.

Without clarity on the opportunity, the boundaries of the request, and how it aligns with your values and priorities, a Deed can quickly deteriorate into a Ditty. When deciding whether to take on a Deed, it's crucial to be intentional and mindful of its purpose and limits. Consider the opportunity cost and what you might have to give up if you commit to the task. Without this careful thought, you risk taking on unnecessary tasks that drain your time and energy for other things. So, proceed with caution and ensure that any Deed you choose truly aligns with what matters to you.

The Ditty-Deciphering Cheat Sheet

Congratulations!

You've navigated your way through the 4-Ds of decision-making: Ditties, Deeds, Duties, and Delights. We know that we've presented you with a lot of questions to remember—so we have a cheat sheet! Next time someone tosses a request your way, run it through the *Ditty Decision Tree* and see where you end up.

Ditty Decision Tree

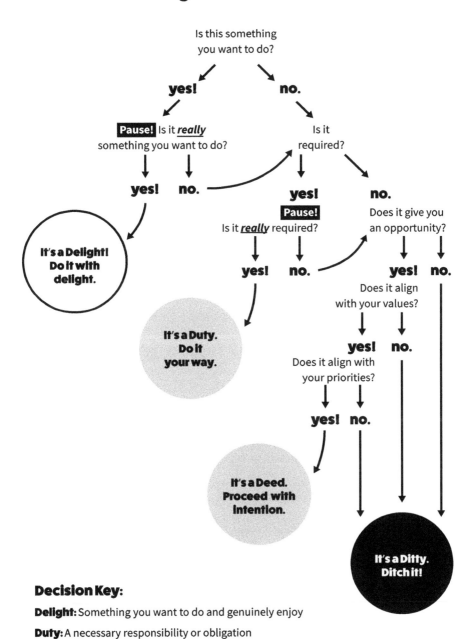

Decision Key:

Delight: Something you want to do and genuinely enjoy

Duty: A necessary responsibility or obligation

Deed: An unwanted task that offers other opportunities

Ditty: Something you neither want nor need to do

Part 1 Ditty-Ditching Duhs

To sum up everything we've just covered, here's a recap of the key insights that we call our "Ditty-Ditching Duhs." You'll find nuggets of wisdom like these at the end of each section to support you as you embark on your own Ditty-Ditching journey.

1. **Decoding Decisions with the 4-Ds:** The key to making intentional choices and focusing on what truly matters is understanding the differences between:
   - Ditties are tasks you neither want nor need to do.
   - Deeds are unwanted tasks that offer other opportunities.
   - Duties are necessary unwanted tasks done out of other commitments.
   - Delights are tasks you want to do and genuinely enjoy.

2. **Socialized to Serve:** Women often take on more Ditties due to gendered socialization that teaches us to be accommodating and put others' needs first. Not every request deserves an automatic "sure, I can do that!" response. Each ask and task is an opportunity to pause and reflect: *Do I really want to do this? Do I really need to do this?*

3. **Seeing and Shedding Ditties...Neo and Glinda Style:** Just like Neo in *The Matrix,* once you start seeing Ditties, you can't unsee them—and that's a good thing![31] But also remember Glinda the Good Witch's wise words: "*You've always had the power, my dear...*"[32] Noticing Ditties is the first step, but knowing you have the power to Ditch them is the key.

4. **There Is Power in the Pause:** One of the most powerful yet underutilized tools in our Ditty-Ditching arsenal is the pause. Whether it's 30 seconds, 30 minutes, 30 hours, or 30 days, taking whatever time you need to reflect on an ask is crucial. Developing this habit can be one of the most impactful steps in your quest to Ditch more Ditties.

PART 2
Decoding the Ditty Dynamics

Deciphering Ditties from Deeds, Duties, and Delights takes discipline. While our "persevere-at-all-times" muscles are strong as women, our "pause-and-reflect" muscles are often weaker from underuse. Taking a moment to ask, *"Is this something I want to do, need to do, and that aligns with my values?"* can mean the difference between picking up another unwanted Ditty and making more time for Delights. As we just explored, pausing is key to Ditching Ditties and making intentional decisions. But there's another important lesson we've learned over the years in our Ditty-Ditching practice, which we'd be remiss not to share:

The pause is necessary, but not sufficient.

While each of those questions posed in the Ditty Decision Tree on page 41 may seem easy enough to answer, we wouldn't be telling you the whole story if we suggested that a simple pause was enough to clarify the choices before us. We must also take a deeper dive into the context of our choices, understanding the socialized tendencies that influence us—especially as women—into accepting unwanted tasks and expectations.

While we may not have received a "How to Be a Woman" playbook at birth, we've been inundated with implicit and explicit messages about how we "should" respond in various situations for centuries. Consider the classic nursery rhyme from the 1820s that still lingers today, reminding us for over two centuries of the expected differences between boys and girls:

What are little boys made of?

Snips, snails

And puppy-dogs' tails

That's what little boys are made of.

What are little girls made of?

Sugar and spice

And everything nice

That's what little girls are made of.[33]

While all our gendered messages haven't been so thoughtfully put into rhymes over the years, they do remain an ever-present soundtrack in our lives. Reflecting on all the "sugar and spice" stuff we've been told throughout our lives, the three of us became deeply curious about what other "ingredients" we've been told are necessary for women. This led us to ask:

Just what is the recipe we've been sold for being a successful woman?

Diving into the theories and research on this topic, there's a wealth of evidence supporting the notion that differentiated gender socialization continues to prevail in our society. What exactly is "differentiated gender socialization," you may ask? To put it simply, our society reinforces different behaviors—beginning in childhood—depending on the perceived biological sex of an individual. As Dr. Shira Tarrant, an expert on sexual politics and contemporary culture, summarizes, "Gender is taught and reinforced through institutional arrangements that tell us how men and women 'should' behave."[34]

The very first "institution" that reinforces gendered behaviors is the one we're born into: our families. With today's trend of over-the-top gender reveal parties, gender differentiation now begins prenatally. Pink or blue cupcakes, balloons, and sparklers signal the baby's gender and set expectations for how we "should" think of, name, dress, and decorate nurseries for babies before they're even born.

As we navigate various institutions in our society—such as educational systems, religious organizations, political arenas, and the economy—men and women receive different messages about what is considered "good" or even "acceptable" behavior.[35] The cultural phenomenon of Greta Gerwig's *Barbie* movie echoed these messages in America Ferrera's monologue that begins with the now iconic declaration *"It is literally impossible to be a woman."*[36] The speech proceeds to highlight the tension between society's often conflicting expectations for women—like being thin but not too thin, successful but not too ambitious, and nurturing but not overly focused on homelife. Interestingly, Gerwig reflected that during filming of this scene, "I was just sobbing, and then I looked around, and I realized everybody's crying on the set. The men are crying too, because they have their own speech they feel they can't ever give. They also have their own painful tightrope to walk."[37]

So women and men get different messages. So what?

These differing messages about what society values in each gender actually have *significant* consequences for both women and men. (Again, fully exploring men's experiences is worthy of a different book.) In our Ditty-Ditching work, it's critical to recognize that the gendered messages we receive as women deeply influence how we see ourselves, interact with others, and make decisions in all areas of our lives.[38] For example, women are celebrated for saying "yes" rather than "no" when asked to do something.[39] Hmmm…might this lead to women agreeing to take on Ditties when they don't really want to?

Just what are these differentiated gender messages we receive as women and the "so what" realities they create for us? See if any of the following sounds familiar to you.

THE MESSAGE…	THE DATA SHOWS THAT…	THE "SO WHAT?" IS…
Girls take care of others.	• Girls spend 40% more time on unpaid household chores than boys, a trend that's found worldwide.[40] • In different-sex relationships, women do around 65% of the household work.[41] • In the workplace, *both* men and women are more likely to ask women to volunteer for "office housework" (i.e., unpaid, non-promotable tasks).[42] • Women are more likely to volunteer for tasks that hinder promotability.[43] • When women refuse extra work, they often receive worse evaluations, fewer promotion recommendations, and are seen as less likable by peers.[44]	As women, we often prioritize others' needs over our own, devoting significant time and energy to care for and please others before ourselves.

THE MESSAGE...	THE DATA SHOWS THAT...	THE "SO WHAT?" IS...
Girls should be seen and not heard.	• In school, girls are more supportive of boys speaking up and taking charge than of other girls doing the same.[45] • At work, men out-talk women even when groups are primarily women; women only speak as much as men in groups when they outnumber them 4:1.[46] • When speaking in public, women's voices are scrutinized more than their male counterparts', more often labeled negatively as being "shrill" or "naggy."[47]	As women, we often don't speak up to voice our ideas, desires, or needs, resulting in us playing a subordinate role to those who do speak up (*hint*: it's the guys who are speaking up!).
Girls should be good, polite, and nice.	• Parents are more likely to use emotional words when speaking with daughters than with sons.[48] • In the workplace, women face negative backlash for expressing anger while men gain higher status for the same behavior.[49] • Girls receive conditional messages that hamper individuation, such as: Be confident but not conceited. Be smart but not a know-it-all. Ambition is good, but trying too hard is bad. Be assertive, but don't upset others.[50]	As women, we often prioritize keeping the peace, often bottling up our emotions and plastering on a smile—even when we don't want to— in order to ensure everyone else is happy.

The three of us have heard these various messages said explicitly to us throughout our own lives, and we suspect that if you're reading this book, you've heard them, too. We particularly enjoy when we get a *"You should really smile"* tossed our way—don't you? Lindsey, a college professor with a Ph.D., was speechless after a colleague once asked her why she'd want a full-time job since she had a husband and children to tend to at home. Taken collectively and repeatedly, these messages create a powerful signal that as women, we're more valued when we act in certain ways.

Internalizing these messages leads women to act and value themselves differently from men. Global mental health statistics illustrate this. For example, a study of nearly one million people across 48 countries found that men have higher self-esteem than women, regardless of culture.[51] As Catherine Allison summarizes in her blog post *Nice Girls Should Be Seen and Not Heard* "Unconsciously or consciously, we've been conditioned from an early age to believe that men are brighter and more brilliant than we are, which could explain why we sometimes struggle to put ourselves or our opinions forward."[52]

The Intersection of Race and Gender

It is important to acknowledge that many of these gendered messages are amplified even more when race is added into the equation.

The women of color who shared stories with us repeatedly echoed the fatigue of shouldering the weight of both gender and race dynamics, often finding themselves as the sole representative of *both* their gender and race in various spaces. Many recounted the struggle to even gain access to these spaces, let alone find solidarity among those who share similar experiences.

Looking at statistics, the numbers are clear: women of color are significantly underrepresented in leadership positions across various industries, comprising only a fraction of top executives and board members. Moreover, the intersection of gender and racial biases often compounds the challenges they face, with studies showing that women of color experience higher rates of discrimination and microaggressions in the workplace compared to their white counterparts.

For example, research shows that women of color are:

→ Asked more often to engage in "helping behaviors" in the workplace than their white counterparts, including spending a substantial amount of time on DEI work that falls outside their formal job responsibilities.[53]

→ Expected to empathize and assist, yet their emotional labor is rarely reciprocated when they're the ones in need.[54]

→ Expected to take on worse assignments than their white male counterparts, hindering their ability to be promoted.[55]

→ Less likely to be perceived as leaders because they're labeled as erratic, irrational, and angry when they express emotions.[56]

→ More likely to feel like an imposter and feel emotionally exhausted by continually working to "code-switch"—or change how they speak, look, and act to conform to the dominant culture.[57]

While the full intersectionality between race and gender is beyond the scope of this book, we invite you to explore Dr. Cathy Royal's work in Quadrant Behavior Theory[58] and books such as Morgan Jerkins', *This Will Be My Undoing: Living at the Intersection of Black, Female, and Feminist in (White) America*,[59] and Mikki Kendall's *Hood Feminism: Notes from the Women That a Movement Forgot*[60] for more on the intersection of race and gender.

Despite increased awareness of gendered socialization and its impact on women's self-esteem and behaviors, these messages remain prevalent today. This is evident in the Pew Research Center's findings summarized below.[61] When *both* men and women were asked, "What traits or characteristics do you think society values most in men and women?" the results showed a striking difference in the top five traits for each gender.

TRAITS MOST VALUED IN...	
MEN	WOMEN
33% Honesty/Morality	35% Physical Attractiveness
23% Professional/Financial success	30% Empathy/Nurturing/Kindness
19% Ambition/Leadership	22% Intelligence
19% Strength/Toughness	14% Honesty/Morality
18% Hard work/Good work ethic	9% Ambition/Leadership

Why do we highlight all this data? It's not to depress us—though, let's be honest, it's a bit disheartening. First, we want to normalize that *"OMG, no wonder I'm so tired!"* feeling that we, you, and every other woman we know has. Yep, let's just take a moment and acknowledge that, as women, we expend a lot of energy on everyone else besides ourselves and that has a toll on our mental and physical well-being. And that moment you just took to acknowledge this fact might be the only moment you take for yourself today—hey, it's a step! Second, we want to raise our awareness of the unique dynamics that we navigate as women every time we face an ask or expectation so that we can make decisions that better serve us versus others.

If we're going to become better Ditchers of Ditties, we need to consider how these messages translate into behavioral patterns that shape our decisions. Drawing upon the research summarized above, as well as our own lived experiences and stories we've heard from women around the world, we've identified what we refer to as the **Ditty Dynamics,** which we define as:

Ditty Dynamic

/'didē/ /dī'namik/ *noun*
1. an internalized gendered socialization message that impacts how we perceive asks made of us
2. a socialized habit that influences why we accept requests made of us when we do not need nor want to do them

We've found that the three most frequent Ditty Dynamics are:

Ditty Dynamic #1: The Persistent Pleaser

Ditty Dynamic #2: The Perfect Pearl

Ditty Dynamic #3: The Self-Doubting Dame

While not an exhaustive list, this trio tends to be the most prevalent in influencing our decision-making and tendencies to pick up Ditties. These dynamics often interact with each other, creating a trifecta of internalized influences that lead us to take on unwanted Ditties. Unpacking and understanding each dynamic provides a starting place for us to become more intentional in navigating our decision-making.

Before we take a closer look at each of these dynamics, however, we want to emphasize that this isn't about diagnosing something "wrong" with us as women…just the opposite! Let's say that again a little louder:

There is nothing wrong with you if you experience Ditty Dynamics!

Exploring these dynamics helps normalize our experiences and reminds us that it's natural to find yourself rooted in these dynamics. Centuries of messages have been whispered in our ears—and sometimes shouted at us in the streets—that we should feel and act certain ways as women. What's important to recognize is that these internalized, gendered messages muddle our clarity in decision-making. Awareness of these dynamics only enhances our ability to make intentional decisions, clarifying what is and isn't a Ditty. Ultimately, this awareness empowers us to Ditch existing Ditties—or even better, to not pick up new ones.

We invite you to get curious about how these dynamics shape your own Ditty identification and decision-making. There's no shame in becoming more cognizant of how and why we act the way we do. It's an opportunity for untangling what is truly "us" versus "this-should-be-us." With that in mind, let's turn to unpacking each of these Ditty Dynamics.

Ditty Dynamic: The Persistent Pleaser

The messages that echo throughout our lives and urge us to take care of others—while always being polite and nice—result in a distinctive dynamic where women work overtime to make others happy. This constant "others-first" effort is a significant reason why, like many women, you probably feel exhausted all the time! Delving into data specifically related to this dynamic, we found that women:

- Are more likely (56% of women vs. 42% of men) to describe themselves as a people-pleaser.[62]

- Score higher than men on "sociotropy," a personality trait characterized by a strong need for social acceptance.[63]

- Who turn down requests at work fare worse in performance evaluations, receive fewer recommendations, and are perceived as less likable than their male colleagues.[64]

Looking at this data, perhaps it's no wonder we tend to say "yes" when asked to do something!

These facts not only piqued our curiosity, but they also resonated with our own experiences. We realized that our own original Ditty story we shared in the Preface was fueled in part by wanting to please others. If you'll recall that story, Mike handed Molly a literal bag and asked her to hold it for him, even though she was beyond busy juggling many other things at that moment. Holding the bag was both unwanted and unnecessary, thus categorizing it as a Ditty in every sense of the word! Yet, what did Miss-I-want-to-take-care-of-others-Molly do in this scenario? She held it amid everything else she was doing.

Why did she do this?

The three of us have spent many conversations trying to unpack this very question. Molly admitted that she didn't want Mike to feel inconvenienced or forced to find another solution. After much discussion, she ultimately said, *"I didn't want him to feel bad or be unhappy with me."* Discovering that nugget of truth was quite an insight for us!

In our conversations with other women, we repeatedly heard similar tales of people-pleasing. Here's one example.

The Ditty Diaries: Jessica's Story

One of my most memorable people-pleasing moments happened last Christmas. My mother-in-law had a long-standing tradition of baking about a million different types of cookies for the holidays. This year, she decided to "graciously" ask for help, and of course, I couldn't say no.

Now, you need to understand that this cookie extravaganza isn't your average bake-a-dozen-and-call-it-a-day affair. We're talking hundreds of cookies, with each batch having its own intricate design and decoration. Think Martha Stewart meets The Great British Bake Off.

So, there I was in her kitchen, with flour up to my elbows, trying to keep up with her relentless pace. Every time I thought we were done, she'd pull out another recipe. "Just one more batch, dear," she'd say with a smile. And like a dutiful daughter-in-law, I'd smile back, nod, and dive into another bowl of dough.

The best part? I don't even like baking. I can whip up a decent cookie if I must, but it's not exactly my idea of a good time. Still, I couldn't bear the thought of disappointing her or, worse, appearing ungrateful for her "generosity" in including me in this cherished family tradition.

As the hours ticked by, I found myself decorating a particularly intricate batch of gingerbread men, complete with tiny icing buttons and little candy eyes. My mother-in-law, ever the perfectionist, hovered over my shoulder, gently correcting my technique. "Try to be more precise with the icing, dear. We want them to look professional."

By the time we finished, it was well past midnight and I was ready to collapse. Yeah, happy holidays!

This story illustrates the quintessential tendency that's so deeply ingrained within many women: the need to please others at the expense of our own happiness. The term "people-pleasing" has been around for centuries, with the earliest use of it tracing all the way back to 1579![65] Today, it's frequently used to describe someone who has an emotional need to please others, often at the expense of their own needs or desires.[66] Building on this centuries-old concept, we'd like to introduce you to our first Ditty Dynamic: The Persistent Pleaser. We define this as:

The Persistent Pleaser

/pər-'si-stənt '/ /plē-zər/ *proper noun*
One who habitually prioritizes pleasing others over her own happiness, often without even realizing it. She works nonstop to gain approval, dodge any hint of discord, and be the ever-accommodating, agreeable wonder woman in every situation, typically leaving everyone pleased but herself.

Even before we had language for it, this dynamic has been around perhaps as long as people have been walking the earth. In fact, many have suggested that it has evolutionary elements associated with it, which perhaps helps explain why it continues to be so prominent in our behaviors today. Psychotherapist Dr. Sharon Marin states:

> *"Our need to please is actually more of a need to belong. And our need to belong was probably written in our DNA millions of years ago. In order to survive, prehistoric (wo) man had to form groups or tribes that offered protection from predators, pooled resources, and shared work. So, if you weren't accepted by the group, there was a high probability that you'd starve to death or get eaten by a saber tooth tiger."*[67]

People-pleasing may have roots back to our how-to-avoid-a-saber-tooth-tiger days, yet it remains a strong instinct even in our can-you-help-me-unjam-the-copy-machine days. And to be clear, we're not saying that all tendencies for people-pleasing are bad. On the contrary, there are many benefits we reap from sowing those pleasing seeds with others. For example, demonstrating prosocial behaviors toward others is something we look for and reward in our children as they develop from egocentric teens into (hopefully) becoming engaged citizens.[68] It's part of healthy human development to recognize that our actions impact others. Indeed, people-pleasing is often the grease that keeps the social wheels turning in all areas of our lives.

For us, the question is:

When does pleasing others become unpleasant for us?

When we spend all our time pleasing others, we forget to add ourselves into the equation. This can result in feelings of depletion and even anger and resentment. Psychotherapist Gavin Sharpe summarizes that people-pleasing "comes at an emotional cost. If I am a habitual people-pleaser, the more time I spend meeting your needs, the less time I spend meeting mine."[69]

You might ask yourself, "How do I know if I'm doing this?" To help answer that question, we've come up with 10 signs of over-peo-ple-pleasing:

1. Your Google Calendar looks like a rainbow explosion from all the events you've agreed to attend.

2. Your phone autocorrects "no" to "yes" because it's so used to you agreeing to everything.

3. You've adopted the phrase "It's fine, I'm fine, everything's fine" as your personal mantra for juggling all the things you've agreed to do.

4. Your idea of a perfect evening involves Netflix, pajamas, and secretly wishing someone would cancel plans with you.

5. You've perfected the art of smiling through gritted teeth and saying, "No problem!" even when it's definitely a problem.

6. Your Spotify playlist is filled with motivational songs like "I Will Survive" and "I Want You to Want Me."

7. You've considered changing your name to "Sure Thing" be-cause that's what you always say.

8. Your biggest fear is not being liked by everyone—including your neighbor's grumpy cat, so you put food out for it.

9. You hold the world record for attending events you have zero interest in.

10. You're always the one still holding the door open for a line of 20 people.

Take a moment and reflect on this list for yourself. Yep, we're inviting you to take another moment for YOU! In all seriousness, how many of these signs resonate with you? Consider how much of your day is focused on ensuring that the needs, wants, and wishes of *others* are granted with your magic wand? How many hours in your precious daily allotment of 24 are devoted to attending to *your* unique desires and needs? Most likely, your day resembles a classic "greater than" and "less than" math expression:

$$\text{My needs} < \text{Everyone else's needs}$$

Again, if you're feeling this way, you're not alone! We regularly feel this way, too. And almost every woman you know has probably felt the pull of people-pleasing, resulting in her putting others' needs before her own at some point. Remember that we've been swimming in a sea of messages our entire lives that suggest women "should" act this way, so this dynamic isn't really surprising. Dr. Teyhou Smyth, therapist and professor at Pepperdine University, sums up our people-pleasing socialization:

> "The pressure that women feel to be people-pleasers is very real. [...] Young girls are told to be quiet and pleasant, to be oriented towards others, to not speak up for what they want, and to please others. These gender-based stereotypes are continuously reinforced in our society in a manner that distinctly disadvantages women."[70]

The next question for us becomes:

How does being The Persistent Pleaser impact our Ditty deciphering and decision-making?

The truth is that this Ditty Dynamic can impact us at each step of our Ditty Decision Tree. Remember that the first step is to ask: "Is this something I *want* to do?" Considering all these messages and the fact that we're socially programmed to worry how others will react if we say "no," it's no wonder this question is hard to answer!

As we internalize the need to please others before ourselves, we're more likely to say "yes" to whatever task, ask, or request comes our way. If we don't untangle our people-pleasing programming, we can easily stumble right out of the gate in our decision-making and assume that we want to do something simply because it will please someone else. Becoming aware of your own people-pleasing tendency is important for navigating intentional decision-making.

A Bite-Size Challenge

To counter the people-pleasing habit, when someone asks you to do something, consider:

→ Will doing this please me?

→ Where am I on my list of people to please?

→ If I say "no" to this, whom will that please?

Ditty Dynamic: The Perfect Pearl

For our next Ditty Dynamic, let's look at more data.

- 44% of women exhibit the trait of self-criticism, compared to 34% of men.[71]

- At work, 38% of women don't feel that they meet the high standards they set themselves, compared with 24% of men.[72]

- When it comes to home and family life, 30% of women feel that they're not meeting the standards they want, compared with 17% of men.[73]

We found these statistics to be both curious and unsurprising, especially as we reflected on our own experiences and those of other women we know and work with. The following are just a few windows into our own challenges with this particular Ditty Dynamic.

The Ditty Diaries: Lindsey's Story

Once I spent two hours of my busy workday personally stuffing and licking envelopes for invitations to an event I was overseeing. Why would someone with a Ph.D. and a million other things to do waste time on this seemingly menial task? Because the person originally assigned to this task messed it up for a previous event, putting the wrong invitation in the wrong envelope. This resulted in one (yes, ONE!) person being upset about receiving a letter with the wrong name on it. Rather than risk the wrath of others feeling "wronged" by a mislabeled letter, I took over the entire production line, meticulously double-checking every envelope to ensure they were done perfectly. It was a Ph.D.-level exercise in perfectionism gone awry! And don't even get me started on the countless hours I've wasted in the time-sucking black hole of making sure the fonts are consistent in PowerPoint presentations...

Have you ever taken over a task because you thought it needed to be done a certain way and you wanted to ensure it was done perfectly? Yeah, we've got about 100 more stories like this! Perfectionism can bubble up in every corner of our lives, as this next story demonstrates.

The Ditty Diaries: Miriam's Story

I often have a perfectionist streak that turns me into a tornado of frantic energy whenever friends or family visit. Picture me racing around the house, scrubbing every corner, fluffing pillows, and acting like a host on a home makeover show. In the past, I've been like the Tasmanian Devil, whirling through the house with a duster in one hand and a vacuum in the other. Even the dog started looking at me funny when I came after her with a feather duster once!

Dog eyerolls or not, I'd convinced myself that if everything wasn't spotless, my guests would be disappointed.

Have you ever felt the need to make everything perfect in your home, office, or even your car when someone's going to see it, fearing that otherwise you'll be judged and found wanting? Again, join the club! And, for those of you who are parents, we know you have many mom-related tales around these dynamics, too, as the following story illustrates.

The Ditty Diaries: Molly's Story

I remember the time I leaned in to ensure my son's hockey team had the perfect personalized posters for a tournament. It all began with an email inviting parents to stay during practice and help make signs for each player's hotel room door for their upcoming hockey tournament.

So, there I was, with five other moms (no dads in sight), huddled around a table with poster board, scissors, paper, and glue. One mom said, "I think we should make posters that look like each of the kids in their jerseys to hang on their hotel room doors at the tournament." Another mom chimed in, "Great idea! Let's start by each making one for our own kids!" Then another mom piped up and added, "Shouldn't we put two different colors on the jerseys, so they look like their actual uniforms instead of just one color?"

I dared to ask, "Won't that take a lot more time? Do you think it's really necessary?"

Let's just say that I was quickly overruled as another mom enthusiastically declared, "These posters are going to help the kids have such a perfect weekend. They'll feel like rock stars with these on their doors with their names and jersey numbers!"

Glorious crafting ensued, two colors and all.

Fast-forward a week later: I'm cleaning up my son's ever-essy room and find the poster on the floor of his closet under a week's worth of dirty clothes. Clearly, he cared deeply about that two-colored poster I spent so much time working on!

I realized then that I had just enacted a true-life encore of a hilarious scene in an actual movie called Bad Moms.[74] *This movie humorously critiques the perfectionism mothers often internalize and reinforce with each other. In one scene, a mom lists a long list of dietary restrictions for a bake sale—including no BPA, MSG, BHA, BHT, sesame, soy, nuts, eggs, milk, butter, salt, sugar, or wheat. Another mom interrupts to confess she's exhausted and done trying to be the perfect mom and is done with these unrealistic expectations.*

If only I had been so bold when asked to make those hockey posters!

Yet another reason women are so tired: we're working so very hard to be perfect at every task before us. Whether it's making presentations just right, chasing dust bunnies out of our house, hosting a social media-worthy dinner party, crafting sparkling posters for the kids…or…or…or…the list is endless. This penchant for perfection leads us to the next Ditty Dynamic—meet The Perfect Pearl.

The Perfect Pearl

/'pər-fikt/ /pərl/ *proper noun*

> One who has internalized the message that she needs to do everything flawlessly to be seen as the best, whether at work or play. Fueled by perfectionism and an endless parade of "shoulds," she often ends up feeling like her tank is running on empty, all while tying perfect bows on things for others.

Is it any wonder that this dynamic is so prevalent in our lives? Again, if we reflect on the messages that we continually receive from the time we're young, research shows that girls get praised by teachers and parents for being "good" or doing something "right," whereas boys are praised for "trying."[75] As a result, girls learn that our value comes when we do things the "right" way, and we actually begin to crave approval for being good.[76]

Just as with people-pleasing, we aren't claiming that striving to do things well is inherently bad. Indeed, delivering things with quality and with attention to detail is a characteristic that is correlated with success on many fronts. Research shows that perfectionists have higher levels of motivation and conscientiousness, leading to beneficial outcomes at work and home. However, the flip side reveals that they also experience higher levels of stress, burnout, and anxiety.[77]

For us, the question is:

When does perfectionism become a perfect pain in the you-know-what?

When we spend our energy ensuring that everything is done right rather than enjoying what we're doing, we can become risk averse to trying new things for fear of failure. Research by Stanford professor Dr. Carol Dweck and her colleagues suggests that because of the "be good" messages we receive, girls often develop a fixed mindset—the belief that one's ability is fixed or static.[78] As Paula Davis, a burnout prevention and stress resilience expert, summarizes:

> "[Girls] avoid challenges, try to look smart, give up easily if they can't be perfect on the first try, and see added effort as fruitless. Meanwhile, young boys who are told to keep trying tend to develop a growth mindset—the belief that ability can be developed. They embrace

challenges, persist during setbacks, and believe that with more effort or repetitions, they can master a task. While not all girls have fixed mindsets and not all boys have growth mindsets, research certainly suggests that the way boys and girls are praised has consequences later in life. Girls stop raising their hands because they don't want to be the only one who doesn't get it or who has a question, and they stop taking as many good risks."[79]

You might ask yourself: "How do I know if I'm being overly perfectionistic?" Here are our top 10 signs of excessive perfectionism:

1. You rewrite texts five times before hitting send.

2. You're convinced that every mistake is going to earn you a big scarlet "M" that will publicly proclaim your imperfection.

3. The phrase "good enough" is not in your vocabulary.

4. You've rewritten sticky notes because the first one wasn't written neatly enough.

5. You're the reigning champion of The Self-Criticism Olympics.

6. You'd rather get a root canal than find a typo in the email you just sent someone.

7. You'd take a hard pass on trying something new rather than subject yourself to the horror of not being instantly brilliant.

8. Delegating tasks to others feels like asking someone to juggle eggs blindfolded; you're convinced they're going to crack something.

9. Your stomach throws an upside-down party whenever plans hit a snag.

10. Your home is spotless, but your mind is cluttered with unrealistic expectations.

How many of these signs resonate with you? Or perhaps you simply feel stuck in a never-ending joke with the punchline:

Knock, knock.

Who's there?

Never.

Never who?

Never good enough!

Ask yourself how often you focus on being the best instead of enjoying what you're doing. Do you ever give 80% or 90% instead of 100%? If you're like us, then "that's good enough" isn't in your vocabulary, and the thought of doing "less than your best" makes you begin to break out in a cold sweat. And then, feeling like nothing is ever good enough makes you invest more time and energy into making it perfect.

Remember, if you feel this way, there's nothing wrong with you. We repeat: There's nothing wrong with you! The Perfect Pearl's shadow stretches long across our lives as women. In their work on *The Confidence Code*, Katty Kay and Claire Shipman recap how study after study shows that as women:

> *"We don't answer questions until we are totally sure of the answer, we don't submit a report until we've edited it ad nauseam, and we don't sign up for that triathlon unless we know we are faster and fitter than is required. We watch our male colleagues take risks, while we hold back until we're sure we are perfectly ready and perfectly qualified. We fixate on our performance at home, at school, at work, at yoga class, even on vacation. We obsess as mothers, as wives, as sisters, as friends, as cooks, as athletes."*[80]

Again, we were curious:

How does being The Perfect Pearl impact our Ditty deciphering and decision-making?

Much like The Persistent Pleaser, this Ditty Dynamic can also come into play at each step of our Ditty Decision Tree. As we hold on to the image that we need to be perfect in the eyes of everyone else, we're more likely to say "yes" to asks that come our way because we don't want to be seen as somehow insufficient or "not good enough." We're also likely to say "yes" to things because we *want* things to be done perfectly and believe if we do them ourselves, we can become mistresses of space and time and ensure perfection in a way that no one else can. Sometimes, we even twist the initial question from "Do I want to do this?" (where the answer may be a clear "no") into "Do I want this done a certain way?" (which makes the answer "yes, so I guess I'll do it"). This twist adds a lot of unwanted Ditties onto our plate over time. Becoming aware of your own Perfect Pearl tendencies is crucial for avoiding unintentional Ditties.

A Bite-Size Challenge

The next time you're faced with a request from someone while you're working to pause your perfectionism, ask yourself:

→ If I say "no" to this, how will that give me more time to perfect the things I really want to be doing?

→ How can I imagine saying "no" to this in the most perfect way ever?

→ If I say "yes" to this, what would "good enough" look like as an outcome?

Ditty Dynamic:
The Self-Doubting Dame

Our next Ditty Dynamic is a close cousin to The Perfect Pearl—related, yet different. To begin, let's again look at some data.

- Men tend to overestimate their abilities while women tend to underestimate them.[81]

- Research shows that 75% of women report having experienced imposter syndrome at some point in their career, and the majority of those women also believe their male counterparts do not experience feelings of self-doubt as much as female leaders do.[82]

- Even AH-mazing women like Maya Angelou have reported feeling like an imposter, saying, *"I have written eleven books, but each time I think, 'Uh oh, they're going to find out now. I've run a game on everybody and they're going to find me out.'"*[83]

These findings did not surprise us as they echoed our experiences of questioning our own competence and confidence. We each have a plethora of stories or times when we were asked to do something that was well within our ability, yet we felt unworthy of the tasks before us. For example:

The Ditty Diaries: Miriam's Story

A while back, I was asked to co-teach a class with a highly regarded thought leader in our field. My immediate reaction was panic. "Why are they asking me to do this?" I thought. "I'm not as skilled as the others who are teaching this." The fear of being found out as "not good enough" washed over me like a tidal wave. I imagined being in front of students with this renowned expert by my side and felt the weight of expectations bearing down on me. My mind raced through all the ways I could mess up, picturing the thought leader shaking their head in disappointment. The more I dwelled on it, the more I felt like an imposter, convinced that everyone would soon realize I didn't belong there.

The Ditty Diaries: Lindsey's Story

I recently found myself doubting my ability to negotiate when buying a car, despite having a master's degree in conflict resolution and having studied negotiation! I had done all the "right" things—conducted extensive research on the car I wanted and its market value, and revisited common negotiation strategies. Yet, I felt anxious and unsure of myself as I stepped into the dealership. As the salesperson presented various options and prices, I second-guessed my prepared counteroffers and feared coming across as inexperienced or being taken advantage of.

Even though I had meticulously studied every detail, my confidence wavered under the pressure. I could feel my palms getting sweaty and my heart racing as I sat across from the salesperson. I kept thinking, "What if I mess this up? What if I overpay?"

Finally, I managed to muster the courage to negotiate a fair price. I felt a rush of relief when the salesperson agreed to my terms. However, as I left the dealership, I couldn't shake the nagging feeling that I could've done better. I kept replaying the conversation in my head, convinced that I didn't handle the negotiation as well as I should've—me with a MASTER'S DEGREE in this work— and wondering if I'd missed out on a better deal or if my alma mater was going to revoke my diploma.

In talking with other women, we heard these *"Uh oh, they're going to find out now"* narratives over and over again, like this story:

The Ditty Diaries: Jamie's Story

I'd been asked to take on the role of Executive Director in my organization. In every practical sense, I had already been acting as the Executive Director for years, oversee-

ing all the executive functions and decision-making within the organization. Yet, when faced with the invitation to formally step into the title, I hesitated and questioned if I was capable of being successful.

As I discussed my doubts with a trusted mentor, she reminded me that I had indeed been acting as the Executive Director—simply without the title—for months. Gradually, I began to realize that perhaps I wasn't so incapable after all. With renewed confidence, I agreed to take on the title officially. This experience showed me how deeply ingrained my doubts could be, even when I had already proven myself capable.

This perpetual perception that we might not be good enough results in the third most common Ditty Dynamic: The Self-Doubting Dame.

The Self-Doubting Dame

/ˈself/ /daʊ.tɪŋ/ /deɪm/ *proper noun*
> One who constantly questions her decisions, self-worth, qualifications, and value. Burdened by the persistent whisper of "Am I good enough?" she frequently second-guesses her abilities, no matter how capable she truly is.

It's perhaps no wonder that women experience high rates of self-doubt, especially in our professional spheres where we often strive to 'fit in' to organizational cultures that have been historically male-dominated. This self-doubt feeling isn't just bound to the boardroom, but can creep into our personal lives as well—which Lindsey's car negotiation story illustrates. Columnist Aimee Lee Ball reflects on the pervasiveness of self-doubt in her article "Why Women Have Low Self-Esteem - How to Feel More Confident":

"When I meet a book editor about a potential publishing contract, I fret about my abilities, discounting a thriving career and a reputation in good standing of more than 20 years. If guests are coming for dinner, I worry that my home won't be pleasing, that my brownies won't merit the caloric expenditure, that the conversation won't be sufficiently scintillating."[84]

Aimee's reflections show just how The Self-Doubting Dame and The Perfect Pearl play together. Building on Miriam's earlier house cleaning tale, imagine her and Aimee together in preparation for company!

Other research has explored how self-confidence has been weaponized against women. In their *Harvard Business Review* article on this topic, Darren Baker and Juliet Borke summarize this issue:

"When women fail to achieve career goals, leaders are prone to attribute it to a lack of self-confidence. And when women demonstrate high levels of confidence through behaviors, such as being extroverted or assertive, they risk overdoing it and, ironically, being perceived as lacking confidence. No matter the outcome, women's lack of career progression is blamed on them, an attack they share with other underrepresented groups. This leads women to beat themselves up, which can weaken self-esteem and, in a downward spiral, further erode self-perceptions of confidence."[85]

Once again, we've crafted our top 10 list of signs that self-doubt might be getting the better of you:

1. You second-guess every decision, from choosing what to wear to ordering at a restaurant.

2. You secretly expect a hidden camera crew to jump out and announce that you've been "pranked" whenever you achieve something.

3. Getting complimented feels like receiving a mystery package from Amazon: unexpected and potentially suspicious.

4. You worry with every minor life hiccup that you'll be un-masked as a failure.

5. You start your sentences with "This might be a silly idea, but..." even when it's a great idea.

6. Your success feels like winning the lottery, except instead of cashing in, you're busy wondering if your ticket is legit.

7. You calculate the tip three times—even after using the calcu-lator—just to make sure it's right.

8. You're like a detective constantly searching for evidence to confirm your self-criticisms.

9. You hesitate to share your opinion in a meeting, even though you know you're well prepared.

10. Fearing the barista's judgment about your ordering abilities, you mentally rehearse ordering coffee at your local café to make sure you don't stumble over "grande" or "latte."

Once again, we invite you to take a moment and reflect on this list for yourself—give yourself at least 60 more seconds of focusing on yourself today! How often do you take full credit for something you did? How often do you let yourself say, "I am a rockin' rock star who rocks things on a regular basis?" Again, if you're anything like us, that mantra isn't anywhere in your inner dialogue...yet!

Don't forget, you're NOT weird if you feel like an imposter some-times—you're once again in good company. In fact, over 70% of all people—men and women—report having imposter feelings at some point in their life.[86] This feeling is so common, we want to emphasize the irreverently perfect sentiment of L.V. Anderson in her article,"Feeling Like an Impostor Is Not a Syndrome", when she wrote, "maybe we should stop calling people who experi-ence impostor syndrome 'people who experience impostor syn-drome' and start calling people who don't experience impostor syndrome 'overconfident weirdos.'"[87]

What we're curious about is:

How does being The Self-Doubting Dame impact our Ditty deciphering and decision-making?

Feelings of self-doubt can come into each step of our Ditty Decision Tree, just like with the other Ditty Dynamics above. Whereas we might think that feeling self-doubt would influence us to say "no" more often, ironically it can have just the opposite impact. As we internalize the feeling of not being good enough, we often want to prove our worth by demonstrating that we can do all the things being asked of us. We become more likely to say "yes" to an ask that comes our way, not necessarily because we want or need to do it, but because we want to show that we can do it.

Take the example of Maureen Zappala, a former propulsion engineer (she's literally a rocket scientist), who shared how her self-doubt propelled her tendency to take on things—dare we say Ditties—that perhaps she didn't need to:

> *"For years I thought NASA only hired me because they needed women. I felt under-qualified and in over my head. I worked long hours to try to prove myself. I was too afraid to ask for help because I thought if I'm really as smart as they think I am, I shouldn't need the help, and I should be able to figure this out on my own."*[88]

We invite you to reflect on a question we've found provocative in our own doubt-fueled decision-making:

When does self-doubt lead us to lean in when we really want to lean out?

In her bestseller *Lean In: Women, Work, and the Will to Lead*, Sheryl Sandberg encourages women to push past their own self-doubt and strive for their best, asking, "Are you striving to achieve, or are you bound by your own limiting thoughts?"[89] Meanwhile, in her bestseller *Lean Out: The Truth about Women, Power and the Workplace*, Marissa Orr argues instead that we shouldn't lean in to dysfunctional systems that continue to point to women as the problem and instead lean out as a way to change the system.[90] So, are we supposed to be leaning in? Leaning out? Just having doubts about whether to lean in or lean out can make us second-guess ourselves!

Both viewpoints can influence whether we pick up Ditties or not. Regardless of when and why we're leaning in or out, we've found that becoming aware of our own Self-Doubting Dame tendencies is crucial for avoiding unintentional Ditties. We need to ensure that we're not miscategorizing Ditties as Duties—and taking on tasks we don't need or want to do—simply because we feel like we have something to prove. Recognizing these tendencies helps us make more intentional choices and focus on what truly matters.

A Bite-Size Challenge

As you work to silence your inner imposter, the next time you face a request, ask yourself:

→ Do I want to say "yes" to this to prove my worth or because I really want to do it?

→ What would a prescription of self-compassion look like here? We take Tylenol for a headache, so what might be the equivalent relief when you feel that imposter itch creeping in?

→ To prevent new imposter episodes, how might you track your wins—even small ones—so you have a record of your AH-mazing accomplishments to counteract that voice of doubt?

We've just unpacked three Ditty Dynamics that might be seriously impacting your life: The Persistent Pleaser, who's always bending over backward to keep everyone happy; The Perfect Pearl, obsessively chasing a flawless, unattainable ideal; and The Self-Doubting Dame, who second-guesses everything she does. Do they sound familiar? We actually hope they do because, just like with Ditties, once you see these dynamics, you can't unsee them. And that's a good thing! This awareness helps you become more intentional, so you can focus on what really matters instead of saying "yes" to everything that comes your way.

Part 2 Ditty-Ditching Duhs

As we wrap up another chunk of info, here's a quick summary of takeaways to carry forward in your own Ditty-Ditching work.

1. **Life Is a Tale of Two Different Scripts:** Even in those early stories of "snips and snails" versus "sugar and spice," men and women receive different societal messages from a young age, which leads to distinct ways of seeing and valuing themselves and ultimately affects how they act. These differing scripts often result in women internalizing the need to please, perfect, and prioritize others over themselves. Recognizing these dynamics is the first step in rewriting your own playbook to Ditch those unwanted Ditties and embrace a life that's truly lived on your own terms.

2. **Experiencing Ditty Dynamics Is Proof That You're Normal:** If you find yourself resonating with any or all these Ditty Dynamics, that means you're in good company! These dynamics aren't a symptom that there's anything wrong with you. They're a normal reaction to the deeply gendered environments that we continue to navigate as women.

3. **Ditty Dynamics Can Create Drama Everywhere in Our Life:** These dynamics can be felt in any sphere of our life. Sometimes you might find that one dynamic shows up more often at work or at home, or sometimes they all show up together in all places! However you experience them, you're not alone! More often than not, your female friend or coworker feels the same way—even if they don't always show it.

4. **Ditty Dynamics Speak Up at Different Times:** You may find that one of the Ditty Dynamics particularly resonates with you over the others. Or you may find that they wax and wane for you at different times in your life. Simply noticing when you're feeling them will help you become a more intentional decision-maker and Ditty Ditcher!

PART 3
Unmasking the Ditty Disguises

Do you feel ready to Ditch some Ditties? You are! But to help ensure you're armed with a full arsenal of Ditty-Ditching devices, we want to share one last secret with you:

Ditties come in all sorts of disguises.

Life would be so much easier if Ditties came with a clear label—or even better, a flashing neon sign that says, "Hello, I'm a Ditty, Ditch me!" Alas, they're much more elusive. Like Halloween trick-or-treaters, Ditties often come knocking on our doorstep in a variety of disguises. Some disguises are simple, making it easy to see the kid behind the costume. Others are much more elaborate, leaving us wondering who just took our last full-size Snickers bar.

What is a Ditty Disguise, you might ask? We define it as:

Ditty Disguise

/ˈdidē/ /dɪsˈgaɪz/ *noun*
1. a request that's sneakily presented as harmless or beneficial, making it hard to recognize as something you don't really want to do
2. a task that appears important at first glance but is actually just a Ditty cleverly masquerading as a genuine priority

Why do we need to recognize these disguises? Ditty Disguises often trigger us into habitual "yes" responses. By spotting these triggers, we can break the cycle and avoid saying yes to things we don't truly want.[91] This awareness helps us see beyond layers of obligation, guilt, or societal expectations, enabling us to respond authentically to the request beneath the mask.

Through our conversations with women around the world, we've heard stories about the myriad of ways Ditties can be disguised. While the following list is not exhaustive by any means, we consider these our top four "most wanted" dastardly Ditty Disguises that need to be unmasked.

Ditty Disguise: The Caped Crusader

About this Disguise:

We've all been there before. Your boss, your coworker, your friend, your partner, your _____ [insert a character from your life here], says, *"I really need you to do this; you're the only person who can."* We think to ourselves: *"Wow! I'm the only person who can do this?!? I mean, I knew I was special, but I guess I'm a superhero after all!"* Before you know it, you find yourself saying "yes" to their request, wrapping yourself up in a cape, and flying off to save the day. If you aren't careful, however, you'll end up spending all your energy leaping tall buildings that you never really wanted to in the first place.

Known Aliases:

- The Obi-Wan Kenobi:[92] *"You're our only hope!"*

- The Compass: *"Only you can guide us in the right direction!"*

- The Life Raft: *"We need you to rescue us!"*

Does this disguise sound familiar to you? Here's a real-life example of how this disguise came knocking on one of our doors.

The Ditty Diaries: Lindsey's Story

I was recently asked to take on an administrative role in my organization. With constant leadership turnover, my department had been experiencing turmoil and they needed someone to step into the vacant Assistant Dean role for stability. The Interim Dean invited me to a "let's-talk-about-the-future-of-the-organization" meeting. Assuming we'd discuss strategies for the upcoming year, I wasn't prepared when she said, "I want you to become our Assistant Dean. Our team is at a crossroads, and we need your special skills. You're the only one who can help us move forward and rebuild confidence."

Wow! Talk about selling an ask! She added, "I don't need your answer now. Think about it over the next week but know that I believe you're critical to our success." I left the meeting with a heightened sense of pride and importance. I always knew I was talented…but saving the entire organization?

For a moment, I imagined saying "yes" and using my Superwoman skills to save the day. However, I quickly realized the role involved tasks I wasn't excited about that would take me away from work I enjoyed. This position was not a promotion but rather simply adding to my existing workload. When I shared the offer with colleagues, each one said, "Oh yeah, she asked us, too, and we both said 'no!'" At that moment, I knew that I couldn't say "yes," and I turned it down.

Lindsey may have avoided being duped by a Ditty Disguise that time, but for every story like this one, we have three others where we—or other women we know—proudly donned our superhero tights. In these instances, we often tried to leap tall buildings only to land flat on our faces holding kryptonite-filled Ditties. Take this story as an example:

The Ditty Diaries: Katie's Story

I once had a friend who asked me to host a last-minute baby shower for her sister. She called me in a panic, saying, "You're the only one who can pull this off! Without you, it'll be a disaster!" She painted such a dire picture that it tugged at my heartstrings, making me feel like the only person who could save the day. The idea of being the Superwoman who swoops in was too tempting to resist, even though my schedule was already packed and I had zero desire to take on the task.

As the day approached, I found myself buried in a mountain of decorations, party favors, and a to-do list that seemed never-ending. I thought, "Why did I agree to this?" But the allure of being the hero kept me going. On the day of the shower, as I scrambled to make everything perfect, I felt the weight of stress and resentment building. "I can't believe I let myself get roped into this," I muttered to myself. All because I couldn't resist the chance to wear my imaginary cape and be everyone's hero.

The Danger of This Disguise:

The Caped Crusader draws its power by playing upon our ego. We want to be needed. We want to be special. We like believing we have special powers that can save the day. This disguise is aided and abetted by The Persistent Pleaser and The Perfect Pearl. Our relentless pursuit of perfection and the ingrained need to please people often lead us down a precarious Caped Crusader path. When asked to "save the day," many of us end up saying "yes" even when our hearts are screaming "no." The fear of disappointing others coupled with our desire to maintain an impeccable image can become a heavy burden. It's a delicate balancing act between the weight of societal expectations and the desire to say "no," leaving us caught between the roles we want to play and the Superwoman role we've been conditioned to play.

Questions for Unmasking This Disguise:

While we may not be able to catch every Ditty wrapped up in the deceptive Caped Crusader mask, pausing to ask ourselves the following questions when presented with a questionable ask may help:

- Is this genuinely something only I can handle, or are they just blowing smoke up my cape to get me to do it?

- What other resources are needed for this to be successful, and are they in place?

- If no one ever knew I did this, would it be worth it?

- Am I only doing this for the accolades I hope I'll receive?

Ditty Disguise: The Golden Ticket

About This Disguise:

Sometimes when you least expect it, someone comes to you with a request wrapped in a seemingly irresistible bow. The packaging on this Ditty is so seductively shiny that we feel the ask is a reward rather than a request. We think to ourselves, *"How can I possibly pass up this opportunity? This is going to really be great for me in the end!"* Fast forward a few months later when the ribbon has lost its luster and the package's shine has begun to fade, and you may just find yourself caught in a task that makes you feel like recycled wrapping paper.

Known Aliases:

- The Stepping Stone: *"This will really help you get ahead."*

- The Resume Builder: *"This will be good for your career."*

- The Magic Key: *"This will help open up other doors for you."*

Recognize this disguise? The trail of Golden Tickets we each have been sold over our lives could win us a hundred trips to Willy Wonka's. Here are two stories about how this sneaky disguise can camouflage a Ditty.

The Ditty Diaries: Roberta's Example

In the early days of my career, a senior colleague asked me to co-lead a major conference with three high-profile international organizations. He promised it would be an historic event and great for my career. Eager to reap the potential rewards of this promise, I didn't pause to consider if I wanted to do it or what a "yes" would mean. Believing it would bring future opportunities, I enthusiastically agreed.

Three months later, I was buried in logistics and inter-organizational politics. I managed everything from big to small details, all on top of my already-full plate of other responsibilities. Ultimately, the event was a success—great attendance, high-profile speakers, positive media—but it drained every ounce of my energy. In fact, I was literally the person left sweeping up the room after the event was done!

In the months that followed, I waited for the promised career-boosting opportunities that never came. Life returned to normal, and I'm not sure anyone even remembers my role in this event—even the person who originally asked me to do it!

The Ditty Diaries: Miranda's Story

Last summer, I was offered what I thought was a "golden ticket" opportunity by a friend. She asked if I would organize and lead a community fundraising event for a local charity. She said, "This will be such a great chance for you to showcase your organizational skills and make connec-

tions with influential people in our community. Plus, it's for a great cause, and it'll look fantastic on your resume!"

Despite my hesitation, I agreed, envisioning the potential benefits. I threw myself into planning the event, spending countless hours coordinating with vendors, rallying volunteers, and managing promotions. The event itself was a success, raising a significant amount of money for the charity.

However, the promised connections and future opportunities never materialized. Instead, I ended up feeling burnt out and underappreciated. The influential community members I was supposed to impress barely remembered my name, and the charity, while grateful, didn't offer any lasting recognition or opportunities. The "golden ticket" I had hoped for turned out to be a lot of extra work without the anticipated rewards.

The Danger of This Disguise:

The Golden Ticket draws its power from our fear of missing out (FOMO). We often get suckered into saying "yes" to these disguised asks because, like buying a lottery ticket, we want to believe in the possibility of a life-changing win. When someone dangles the promise of good things if we just do one little (or big) thing, it's easy for us to get drawn in by the allure, even when the odds are seriously stacked against us. If you aren't careful, however, you'll end up scratching off a winning ticket for someone else—and cleaning up the confetti from their celebration party to boot.

The Self-Doubting Dame often conspires with this disguise. That nagging feeling of self-doubt can be a relentless companion, especially when we're faced with an enticing Golden Ticket-like opportunity. For many women, this feeling becomes a double-edged sword. The fear of missing out on a chance to prove ourselves or to validate our abilities often propels us to say "yes" even when we may not truly want to do the work at hand. It's a complex dance, one where self-doubt whispers in our ears, convincing us that this is our chance to shine, while our genuine desires quietly wait in the wings. Balancing the need for validation with our authentic wants can be an intricate struggle that often leads us down a path where we end up with Golden Tickets that look much less shiny in the light of day.

Questions for Unmasking This Disguise:

While we wish we could say that we've arrived at a place of awareness and that this disguise has lost its ability to trick us, it still does from time to time. We've found that asking the following questions is useful in helping us see behind the shine of the Golden Ticket to ensure we're not getting fooled into planning someone else's party!

- If there isn't a payoff for me at the end of this work, would I still want to do it?
- If it's such a great opportunity, why don't they want to do it?
- Will there be other opportunities like this in the future if I pass on this one?

Ditty Disguise: The Hot Potato

About This Disguise:

Often, there are tasks in our organizations, our communities, and even in our families that no one wants to do. These are the orphaned Ditties that get passed around like the childhood game of hot potato. Suddenly the music stops, and we look down to see that we're holding the bag no one wants. We think to ourselves, *"Well, this has to be done, and I guess it's my turn to do it."* We bite the bullet and take on the Ditty. Sometimes, however, people forget to turn the music back on, and we're left holding that potato until it's cold and sprouting new Ditties of its own.

Known Aliases:

- The Short Stick: *"Someone has to do this, let's draw straws."*
- The Un-Merry-Go-Round: *"We all have to do this eventually; it's your turn."*

- The Not-It: *[Silence…finger on nose]*

Have you ever found yourself with one of these potatoes? From organizing office parties that no one really cares about to taking care of your roommate's high-maintenance pet while they're on vacation, we've all found ourselves holding The Hot Potato no one else wants. Hot Potatoes pop up in all spheres of our lives—from the dorm room to the boardroom to the living room! Here's one example.

The Ditty Diaries: Molly's Story

Last year, I was contemplating hosting our family's annual holiday gathering. Every year, my siblings and their families like to come together for our annual holiday festivities, but nobody ever wants to be left holding the tray of roasted responsibilities for planning and organizing the event. When they turned to me once again, asking me to hone my party planning skills and saying, "No one else wants to plan it," I realized that the holiday hosting role had turned into a Hot Potato with a side of cold turkey.

For a moment, I was ready to suck up my angst and agree, but then it hit me: My "yes" would be a gateway to hosting not just this year but for years to come. With clarity and conviction, I said, "If no one wants to plan it, then perhaps we shouldn't do it." Somewhat surprised, one of my siblings stepped up and agreed to host at her house instead. So, at least this time, the Hot Potato was passed on.

Avoiding The Hot Potato hasn't always been as lucky for us as it was for Molly. We've heard numerous stories from women that highlighted how they found themselves being the ones who:

- Took the notes in the meeting when no one else wanted to.

- Sent out the calendar invitations for a meeting they weren't leading.

- Have been the only one to bring food to events.

- Tidied up shared spaces—at work and home.

- Reviewed and edited (even created) documents they weren't responsible for.

- Organized a party for work, home, and everywhere else in between.

The Danger of This Disguise:

The Hot Potato draws its power from a woman's desire to be a good team player. We want the merit badge "plays-well-with-others" stitched onto our sash of successes. We believe that life is fair and that if we take one for the team now, the team will pitch in and help us in the future. Take, for example, this story we heard:

The Ditty Diaries: Claire's Story

I remember when my boss decided to jet off on vacation at the worst possible time for the office. We were swamped with deadlines and critical projects, but he didn't seem to care. Naturally, he asked me to take care of a mountain of extra responsibilities before leaving.

One afternoon, I confided in a colleague, "I know I shouldn't be doing all this work for him. It's not fair, but maybe if I do, it'll give me a leg up when negotiating my role next year."

My colleague looked at me with raised eyebrows and said, "Don't hold your breath on that. Institutions have short memories. Your good deed today will likely be forgotten by tomorrow, let alone next year."

Despite her advice, I plunged into the work, tackling everything from managing meetings to sorting through endless email chains. Every day, I stayed late, my desk lamp burning long after everyone else had gone home.

Weeks passed, and my boss returned from his sun-soaked holiday, blissfully unaware of the chaos he'd left behind. He didn't even really acknowledge the extra work I'd done.

When it came time to discuss my role for the next year, I realized my colleague's warning had been spot on. My boss had completely forgotten the mountain of extra work I had shouldered. The negotiations didn't go as I'd hoped, and the leg up I thought I'd gain was nowhere in sight. This experience taught me a tough lesson about the fleeting nature of recognition in the workplace.

We've seen over and over that if you're not careful, folks forget all about the potatoes you're holding—and they often ask you to juggle a few more root vegetables no one else wanted, leaving you with a real Ditty smorgasbord.

The Persistent Pleaser and The Perfect Pearl exacerbate the power of The Hot Potato. We worry that saying "no" might tarnish our reputation as accommodating and helpful, thus resulting in committing a cardinal sin of womanhood: *NOT* perfectly pleasing someone! Can you imagine?!? Consequently, when handed a Hot Potato task that no one else is willing to touch, we find ourselves reluctantly accepting the challenge. The fear of appearing uncooperative or unsupportive can outweigh our personal reservations. So, we grasp the searing Hot Potato, not because we want to, but because we believe it's expected of us. Inadvertently, we sometimes get burned from holding an unwanted veggie that should have been left buried in the ground.

Questions for Unmasking This Disguise:

The next time you get a whiff that an ask may just be a Hot Potato in disguise, ask yourself:

- If no one wants to do a task, can I revisit the task itself? Does it still need to be done or perhaps changed?

- What are the clear parameters around this potato (i.e., time commitment, expiration date, etc.)?

- What will be removed from my plate to make room for this new potato?

Ditty Disguise: The Veiled Threat

About This Disguise:

One of the scariest disguises that comes knocking on our door is The Veiled Threat, asking, *"Treat or TRICK?"* These are those times when coworkers, bosses, friends, or family members ask us to do something with the subtle—or perhaps not so subtle— implication that if we don't do it, something catastrophic might happen. We think to ourselves, *"Well, I don't want ___ [fill in the blank for whatever horrible trick is being threatened] to happen, so I guess I better do this!"* Next thing we know, we're being strong-armed into doing other Ditties under the same guise.

Known Aliases:

- The "Or Else": *"You better do this or else … [fill in something scary]."*

- The Apocalyptic Movie: *"If you don't do this, everything will fall apart."*

- The Terminator: *"You need to do this if you want to survive."*

While this disguise has fortunately been the least frequent one we've experienced, when it does show up, it can be quite jarring. For an example of this disguise, we return to the story we shared in Part 1 where Molly was asked to be president of a local volunteer board.

The Ditty Diaries: Molly's Story…Continued

As you already know, I initially said "yes" to taking on the role—but upon further reflection, I realized part of the reason I agreed was because it was delivered as a Veiled Threat. The current leadership approached me with not just a request but an implied implosion of something I deeply cared about if I didn't step up. They said, "If you don't take on the president role, our entire 30-year-old organization might fold." Whoa! The ask packs a little more punch when put that way, right?

This framing extended beyond the appeal of being a hero like a Caped Crusader and introduced the ominous suggestion of potential danger if I didn't step up, subtly assigning blame to me for a disaster that hadn't even occurred yet. Feeling the weight of this Veiled Threat, I agreed to pick up the mantle and serve as president. Shortly after taking on the role, I recognized it as a Ditty, yet I persisted...for eight long years!

Veiled Threats aren't limited to the professional world; they often pop up in our personal lives, too. Family and friends—who know exactly what buttons to push—can make us feel like we're the only thing standing between triumph and catastrophe. See if this story sounds at all familiar to you.

The Ditty Diaries: Miriam's Story

Every holiday gathering, it's the same story. A family member inevitably asks me to make this special dish that I'm tired of making. It feels like a Veiled Threat every time. The unspoken message is clear: If I don't make this dish, my family will be disappointed. They expect it, they always want it, and without it, the holidays will be ruined and life as we know it will end. So, I always end up making the stupid dish, even though I'd much rather spend my time cooking something new that I actually might enjoy. I've imagined the disappointment on their faces if I dare to bring something else, and I can just hear their gasps of "But where's THE dish?" So, I end up toiling away in the kitchen over a recipe I wish I could let go, just to keep the peace and avoid an anticipated family holiday apocalypse.

Molly and Miriam's stories are both classic examples of how implied ominous pressure and sense of responsibility can cloud our judgment, making it harder to recognize when we're being manipulated by these subtle threats. They provide a valuable lesson in learning to pause, reflect, and consider the true motivations behind our decisions. All's well that ends well, though, right? The good news is that Molly recently passed the baton on to a new leader—without any menacing threats. We will return to the details of how she Ditched this particular Ditty in Part 5 when we explore how to scale your "no"—even if it's delivered years after you originally said "yes".

The Danger of This Disguise:

The Veiled Threat draws its power from our survival instinct. Thanks to the fact that our ancestors spent their days running from grizzly bears and other dangers, our brains are hardwired to protect us from anything scary. This is especially true for women; we believe we need to prevent our demise by avoiding or neutralizing danger. But if you're not careful, you might waste all your energy running from a gummy bear you thought was a grizzly.

This ingrained reaction is further heightened by the gendered socialization we explored in Part 2, which teaches women to prioritize harmony and avoid conflict. The Persistent Pleaser and The Perfect Pearl dynamics make it challenging to unmask these Veiled Threats for the Ditties they are. Women often say "yes" in these situations out of fear of being disliked or seen as less than perfect.

We also fear being cast as the villain if we refuse. This can feel particularly detrimental because societal expectations pressure women to be nurturing, accommodating, and agreeable. When we defy these roles, we risk being labeled as difficult or unlikable, which can damage our relationships. This fear of negative judgment reinforces our socialized compulsion to please, making it harder to recognize and resist these pressures. When this disguise appears, it's like entering a carnival funhouse where distorted mirrors elongate our obligations and warp our boundaries, leading us to take on responsibilities out of fear rather than genuine desire.

Strategies for Unmasking This Disguise:

- What is the *worst* thing that would really happen if I didn't do this?

- What is the *best* thing that could happen if I don't do this?

- If the request is coming in the form of a threat, is this someone I even want to be dealing with?

A Bite-Size Challenge

Which Ditty Disguise is your kryptonite—the one that lures you in most often to saying, "yes"? (Feel free to check more than one if needed!)

☐ The Caped Crusader

☐ The Hot Potato

☐ The Golden Ticket

☐ The Veiled Threat

What is one question you will ask to unmask this disguise the next time it appears?

Unmasking each of these Ditty Disguises brings significant benefits to our Ditty-Ditching journeys. By unpacking an ask and understanding its true nature, we avoid being inadvertently duped into saying "yes" to tasks that drain our energy and time. Ultimately, recognizing these disguises allows us to make intentional, purposeful choices and sidestep Ditties, no matter how they're wrapped.

Part 3 Ditty-Ditching Duhs

The Caped Crusader, The Golden Ticket, The Hot Potato, and The Veiled Threat are some of the dastardliest Ditty Disguises we've unmasked in our own lives. Here are some important insights to help you unmask these and other disguises your Ditties may wear.

1. **Knowing Is Half the Battle:** Acknowledging that Ditties often disguise themselves in seemingly innocuous forms is an important step in your Ditching journey. They may appear as well-intentioned requests, forced obligations, or even opportunities for growth. To unmask them, we must learn to discern when something is a genuine alignment with personal values and desires versus when it's a concealed Ditty, wrapped up with a bow that can otherwise be quite alluring.

2. **Enlist Ditching-Detective Allies:** Sometimes it takes more than your two eyes to unmask a Ditty Disguise. You don't need to be alone in the battle against disguised obligations. Reach out to friends, mentors, or support groups for their insight and wisdom. Sharing your dilemmas and seeking advice can bring fresh perspectives that can help expose those cleverly disguised Ditties. Other people can often see through the disguises when you're too close to unravel them yourself.

3. **Listen to Your Instincts:** Trust your inner voice—you know, that little voice we often tell to be quiet while we say "yes" to something we don't really want to do. If something doesn't sit right with you, if saying "yes" feels heavy or gives you even a moment of hesitation, it might be a disguised Ditty in your hands. There is significant research today to suggest that your intuition is just your lightning-fast intelligence at work![93] Pay attention to your gut feeling as it often knows when an ask isn't truly aligned with your wants.

90

PART 4
The Ultimate Question: What Do You REALLY Want?

What do you want?

These four simple words comprise a question that seems like it should be so easy to answer. But trying to figure out what you want sometimes feels like you're being handed the menu at an ice cream parlor with a hundred flavors, and you're expected to pick just one. Should you go for the classic vanilla of career success or maybe a swirl of personal fulfillment? Oh, but don't forget the sprinkles of family happiness and the bonus whipped cream of enriching hobbies!

What do you want?

Somehow, we hear this question and it's as if we're being handed a binding contract for the rest of our lives. Or perhaps, after a lifetime of trying to win the *People-Pleaser of the Year Award*, considering our own wants feels like cheating. Yet, step one in determining if something is a Ditty is asking yourself if it's something you want to do. Without clarity about what we want, we risk being reactive—like a boat without a rudder, easily blown off course by the currents and tides and tricked by those dastardly Ditty Disguises.

So, we'll ask again, Spice Girls-style this time:[94]

WHAT DO YOU WANT, WHAT DO YOU REALLY, REALLY WANT?

Trying to crack this question for ourselves, we've grilled friends and loved ones, turned over every rock, and devoured every self-help article out there. But we finally realized that no matter how much we ask others, the answer is perhaps not "out there" to be found. Rather, to answer this elusive question, we need to travel to that final frontier that we rarely ever visit—inward into our own head and heart. Talk about uncharted territory for us!

To begin this interpersonal journey, we first must spend time exploring another question:

Why is "What Do You Want?" such a hard question?

Unpacking this requires us to revisit the differentiated gender socialization research that helped us pinpoint the origins of The Persistent Pleaser, The Perfect Pearl, and The Self-Doubting Dame tendencies. As we explored in Part 2, women have been conditioned for generations to be the world's most attentive mindreaders, constantly attending to what others want or need. Knowing what others want—and tending to those wants—is something that we've long been rewarded for.

From a young age, societal expectations have thrust upon women the responsibility of nurturing others, whether it's family members, friends, or colleagues. Consequently, we've become adept at tuning into the needs of those around us, often at the expense of neglecting our own. Unfortunately, this incessant nurturing role often eclipses our ability to even identify and articulate our own wants and needs. While our learned Persistent Pleaser and Perfect Pearl tendencies give us near magical abilities to know what everyone around us wants, asking ourselves what we want can feel like trying to read a book written in invisible ink. We've simply not exercised the same mental muscles to consider our wants like we do for others. Consider this illustrative tale that shows just how challenging the question "What do you want?" is in our lives.

The Ditty Diaries: Lexi's Story

Whenever I go out to eat with friends, the simple act of ordering at a restaurant feels like a monumental decision. As soon as the waiter arrives and my friends turn to me and ask, "What do you want?" I can feel the pressure mounting.

I know they're looking to share, and I don't want to be the one to suggest something that nobody else will enjoy. Should I go for the classic burger that's usually a safe bet, or should I suggest the adventurous seafood platter that might be hit or miss?

My mind races through the options, imagining their reactions to each choice. I can already hear someone saying, "Oh, I'm not really in the mood for that," or another friend politely trying to hide their disappointment.

So, I hesitate, trying to gauge everyone's preferences while second-guessing my own. I end up mumbling something like "Maybe the nachos? But I'm good with whatever you all want," hoping they'll take the reins and choose something universally loved.

This tiny moment of decision-making, which should be straightforward and enjoyable, often turns into a mini-episode of angst for me—all because I want everyone to be happy and satisfied with what we order.

This story resonated with the three of us so much that we've adopted a mantra for when we go out to eat: "Order what you want!" We remind each other of this before the waiter even arrives.

As women, our habitual focus on tending to the emotional and physical well-being of others can create a blind spot when it comes to recognizing our own needs. This blind spot is reinforced by the ingrained notion that selflessness is a female virtue, perpetuating the belief that prioritizing our own needs is selfish or indulgent. We live in what has been referred to as "the culture of female service." In her article "Why Do Women Find It So Difficult to Put Themselves First?", therapist and expert in mother-daughter relationships Rosjke Hasseldine elaborates on this concept:

> *"The cultural beliefs that we have about how females are the nurturing gender, and that it is a woman's role and duty to care for and nurture their family and community, without needing care in return."[95]*

In other words, women are taught to think that our value depends on our capacity to prioritize others' needs over our own, frequently relinquishing our own wants along the way. If our lives were an airplane flight, the pre-flight announcement would sound like this:

> *In the unlikely event of a sudden drop in cabin pressure, we kindly ask all women aboard to ensure the safety of others by immediately attending to everyone else's oxygen needs before your own. Remember, prioritizing the oxygen masks of your fellow passengers is not only a gesture of goodwill but also a fantastic opportunity to practice your multitasking skills. We trust you'll find a way to juggle everyone's safety while maintaining your usual grace and charm. And if time permits, after everyone else is set, feel free to take a moment to catch your breath before assisting yourself. Thank you for flying with us!*

Reflecting on how an internalized feminine narrative of service has echoed across the generations, Hasseldine further states:

> *"This mindset has created [a] generational pattern of women's unacknowledged needs. It has created a pattern of self-neglect that our mothers and grandmothers learned to tolerate and normalize, because they did not know anything different."[96]*

This intergenerational cultural narrative fuels feelings of guilt and shame around acknowledging personal needs, leading women to suppress or ignore our own wants and desires in favor of fulfilling perceived obligations to others. The implications of focusing on everyone else's needs above our own have real impacts on our lives. For example, research has shown that:

- Our cultural tendency to reward women for being "perpetually pleasant, self-sacrificing, and emotionally in control" may be linked to negative health outcomes for women.[97]

- Self-silencing—or the "tendency to engage in compulsive caretaking, people-pleasing, and not expressing oneself"—is more prevalent in women and is linked to not only increased physical illnesses but also less satisfying relationships.[98]

- Mothers, in particular, hold a hidden mental load of tending to others—which includes "anticipating (others') needs, identifying options, deciding among the options, and then monitoring the results," and leads to them being more stressed, extra-stretched, and less happy than fathers, especially if they are also working.[99]

And perhaps the cherry on top of the "help-others-before-yourself" cake recipe that has been passed down through generations is the fact that societal norms often equate femininity with passivity and compliance, further discouraging women's assertiveness and self-advocacy. Remember that Pew Research Center data we referred to in Part 2? When asked about the characteristics our society values most in women, "empathy/nurturing/kindness" was the second most valued trait—following behind that other all-important female trait of "physical attractiveness."[100]

Message received: We need to help others and look nice while doing it—got it! This reminds us of a famous quote about Ginger Rogers and Fred Astaire: "Sure, he was great, but don't forget that Ginger Rogers did everything he did...backwards and in high heels."[101]

Imagine our society as a movie; the casting director would likely post something like:

Casting Call: The Ideal Woman

Character Description:

We're seeking a bubbly, attractive female lead who effortlessly juggles a high-powered career, a picture-perfect family, and an active social life. Must exude charm and femininity while remaining approachable and relatable to our target audience. Ideal candidate will possess an innate talent for multitasking, flawlessly handling family, work, and social obligations, all without complaint. Experience with baking cookies, going to yoga classes, and organizing meetings is a plus. This role requires impeccable fashion sense, a flawless smile, and the ability to gracefully navigate awkward situations with humor and grace. Applicants should embody the epitome of beauty, brains, and benevolence.

Even when we don't want to try out for this role, we can experience repercussions when we fail to embody it. Going against traditional gender expectations can lead to feelings of "gender role strain" within ourselves.[102] This is the inner struggle we face when we don't quite fit the roles society expects based on our gender. This strain often manifests as guilt, shame, fear, and just plain old stress. It's that nagging guilt that we're letting others down by not conforming, the fear of being judged or ostracized, and the overwhelming stress of trying to juggle conflicting expectations. It's like wearing a one-size-fits-all costume that's clearly a bad fit, leaving us feeling uncomfortable and out of place.

Beyond the internal turmoil we may feel when we go against expected gender roles, there can be external repercussions as well. When we step out of expected gender roles, we can get typecast very quickly. You likely know the new characters we're slapped with. They go something like:

Casting Call: Non-Ideal Women

Description of Possible Characters:

- **The Bossy Bitch:** Assertive, ambitious, and highly skilled but faces rejection and disdain for her confidence and directness. Must have a "resting bitch face" that conveys the personal challenges of being ostracized for defying gender norms, turning ambition and self-confidence into traits that make others uncomfortable.

- **The Drama Queen:** Must be able to cry on cue and oscillate between laughter and tears within seconds. Wears her heart on her sleeve, turning every stubbed toe into a Shakespearean tragedy. Takes everything personally, interpreting even slight comments as deep insults. Known for dramatic exits, tearful confessions, and turning any conversation into a therapy session.

- **The Nagging Ninny:** Should excel at delivering lines that remind others about their forgotten chores, deadlines, and life choices. This character's favorite accessory is a wagging finger, and she never misses the chance to give a stern lecture, complete with a disapproving glare.

It's like there's this unwritten rulebook for how women should act, and when we deviate from it, things can get awkward and uncomfortable for everyone. Research shows that women can be the victims of a double-bind gender bias called the "descriptive and prescriptive bias."[103] Descriptive bias is about labeling people based on who they are, while prescriptive bias tells them how they should act based on those labels. Here are but a few of the adjectives we've been labeled with when we dared to step out of the quintessential female role of the caring-for-others-above-self:

We wish we could simply say, "Sticks and stones will break our bones, but words will never hurt us." However, we wouldn't be honest with you (or ourselves) if we didn't admit that these labels can have serious repercussions, affecting how we feel about ourselves and how we're perceived—and ultimately treated—by others. These labels can stick with us, impacting us in many ways. And while men can also experience gender strain and pushback for not adhering to their gender roles, the stakes for staying in our "assigned" role are often higher for women. Stepping outside of traditional gender norms can impact not only our social standing but also our well-being. Even our physical safety can also become a concern. Women who defy societal expectations may face backlash, harassment, and in extreme cases, even unsafe environments. The fear of these repercussions can be paralyzing, adding layers of stress and anxiety to the already challenging task of navigating our true desires and goals.

The prescriptive expectations for women have an impact in every sphere of our lives, but especially in the workplace. Since Dr. Virginia Shein's studies in the 1970s, research has consistently shown a "think manager-think male" culture, indicating that society commonly perceives a "leader" or "manager" as male or having masculine traits.[104] These prescriptive biases literally stop us from seeing women as leaders.[105] As a result, women face a *double bind* where they must try to balance being assertive enough to lead effectively with not being so assertive that they're labeled negatively or seen as unlikable.[106] Think of it as trying to dance to two different tunes at the same time, leading to a lot of missteps and stepped-on toes. Just imagine the drama that would have ensued if Ginger had tried to lead Fred around the dance floor!

Again, we don't share all this research to be a Debbie Downer. Rather, we want to explain and normalize why answering "What do you want?" can be so challenging for us as women. You're not alone if the answer to this question isn't immediately clear. There's nothing wrong with you if you don't have an answer, or if you've never even paused to ask yourself the question. There are many, many reasons—as noted above—why both the question and the answer can feel elusive and foreign.

But we wouldn't share all of this without some good news as well!

The good news is that we can begin to decipher our own desires by giving ourselves the same gift of attention and intention we give others. So we invite you to buckle up and dive into clarifying what you want…what you really, really want.

Getting Essential About Your Essentials

If Ditties are those obligations filled with other people's stuff that we don't want nor need to carry, we need a parallel concept to refer to the things that matter to us and that we actually *want* to carry around with us. We call these things our Essentials.

Essentials

/ə'sen(t)SH(ə)ls/ *noun (plural)*
1. something that is absolutely necessary and indispensable to you
2. a fundamental element or characteristic of who you are and what matters most to you

Getting essential about our Essentials is like having Marie Kondo, the queen of decluttering, help us with our priorities—it's all about identifying what truly sparks joy and meaning in our lives. By letting go of others' needs and shedding the unnecessary "shoulds" cluttering our minds like incessant cobwebs, we create space for the things that really matter to us.

We suspect that you know what your "shoulds" are. For us, they include things like:

- *I should* want to help this person.

- *I should* step up and make sure this happens.

- *I should* be able to bake Pinterest-worthy cakes.

- *I should* keep my emotions in check.

- *I should* always be helpful.

- *I should* be able to manage my inbox with the precision of a surgeon.

- *I should* remember everyone's birthday.

- *I should* handle everything on my own.

- *I should* always be available for family and friends.

- *I should* excel without complaining.

- *I should* be able to find 10 more hours in the day to do everything for everyone.

Are you ready to start letting go of your "shoulds" and embracing what you truly want? To begin, imagine you're going on a month-long trip across the country with only one carry-on bag. It's probably safe to assume that you can quickly generate a list of your travel "essentials"—all those things that you'll make sure will find their way into your carry-on bag, no matter what.

Try it. What would be the five items that you'd unquestionably pack as your essentials for such a trip?

Now, see if you can list the five most Essential things in your life; the stuff (which could be people, experiences, values, etc.) that you prioritize over everything else. Can you name them as quickly?

You can probably generate a long list of things that matter to you, but we're not talking about *all* the things that you care about. We're talking about your core, fundamental Essentials. The things that guide you when making decisions, the things you'd sacrifice other things for, the things that are truly *essential* to you.

Don't worry if you can't; most of us don't spend much time reflecting on these things. Maybe this is the first time you're giving yourself even a few moments to pause and consider the question:

In the carry-on bag of life, what essentials would you pack?

We struggled with this question ourselves as we sought to become clearer on what Ditties we wanted to Ditch. We went back over the myriad of discovering-your-personal-values exercises that we had each done over the years. We turned to the internet and got lost in Google rabbit holes, searching for advice on search terms like *"How to know what you want"* and *"Getting clarity on what matters most."* Much of this searching resulted in advice that felt circular, reinforcing the need to figure out what was meaningful without concrete suggestions on how to actually do it. Something akin to: *How to get clear on what matters to you… Step 1: Get clear on what matters to you.*

Very helpful.

Ultimately, we realized that perhaps we needed to stop asking others—even the all-knowing Google—to help us figure out our Essentials and actually do the introspective work ourselves. (You knew this was coming!)

While we're not so arrogant as to believe that there's only one way to figure out your Essentials, we've come up with five steps that have helped us personally dive into that fundamental question: What do we really want?

Step 1: Learn Your ABCDEs

To start off, we recognized that we don't just have one thing that matters to us. Rather, our lives are made up of a diverse range of essential elements, much like Maslow's hierarchy of needs.[107] Maslow's theory, which is still highly popular today, highlights various motivating factors that we have as humans, including physiological, safety, relational, self-esteem, and self-actualization needs. While modern views have evolved since Maslow, many current motivation theories agree that we try to meet different needs in our lives.[108] Thus, inspired by Maslow's classic framework—but with a modern twist—we reimagined our needs as five different types of Essentials in our lives, which we fondly refer to as our ABCDEs!

Our Essentials

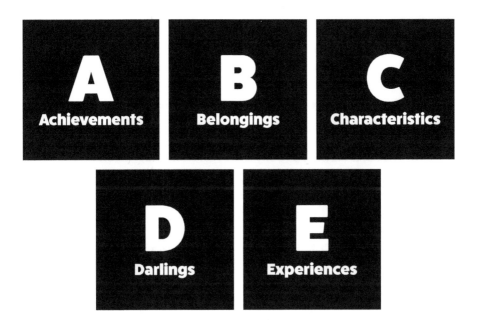

A = Achievements: The impacts we most want to be remembered for; the legacy work we want to leave behind.

B = Belongings: The material possessions that matter most to us; the items that have the most value to us for extrinsic or intrinsic reasons.

C = Characteristics: The personal attributes that matter most to us; our ways of being, or "how" we want to show up in the world around other people.

D = Darlings: The people who are most dear to us; those individuals whom we'd drop everything for and/or whom we consider when making decisions in our lives.

E = Experiences: The activities that we engage in that bring us joy; the way we most enjoy spending our time.

Step 2: Start With the End in Mind... Literally!

Next, to help us get clear on what's truly essential for us, we leaned into the classic adage: "Start with the end in mind." And, in that spirit, we went to the end—literally. We imagined that if our life was a story, what did we want our tale to be when it was all said and done? This may seem a bit morose, but...

> **NEWSFLASH #2:** We really only have so many years (surprise!). And no matter how much we distract ourselves from that reality, every day we're here is an opportunity to write the life story we'll want to celebrate when our days are done.

So, with the literal end in mind, we asked ourselves five questions to help us uncover our Essentials in each of these areas:

ESSENTIAL	QUESTION FOR CLARIFYING
Achievements	At my retirement party, what are the three things I'll have done that I want people to celebrate?
Belongings	If my house was on fire and I only had 60 seconds to get out, what three items would I grab?
Characteristics	At my funeral, what are the three words I hope people use to describe me?
Darlings	If I was on a plane that was crashing, who are the three people I'd call?
Experiences	If I were given three months to live, what three experiences would I prioritize?

A Bite-Size Challenge

We invite you to explore these five questions yourself, with a very important caveat in mind. When you answer them, consider the practice of the **PAUSE** we discussed in Part 1. For each answer you give, ask yourself: *"Is it really?"* Are you answering truthfully or in ways you think you **should** answer if another person stumbled upon your list? We know you're secretly worried your partner, mom, coworker, or best friend might discover this, or perhaps magically read your mind while you're answering these questions. But imagine for just a moment that no one was **ever** going to uncover your responses and answer the questions with that freedom in mind!

Step 3: Sprinkle Your Essentials Everywhere

Once you've identified your essential ABCDEs, the fun part kicks in as you figure out how to sprinkle them throughout your life in more intentional ways. Think of it like adding your favorite seasoning to an everything bagel—you want those Essential elements everywhere! Picture doing things like:

- Crafting your "Essential Mornings," where even just five minutes are dedicated to what truly matters to you.

- Winding down each day with your "Essential Evenings" that include rituals or hobbies to help you unwind.

- Creating "Essential Weekends" that involve doing things you enjoy.

- Curating "Essential Routines" that bring moments of joy into your daily grind.

- Designing "Essential Workspaces" that spark your energy.

- Hosting "Essential Celebrations" that reflect your valued traditions with people you love.

- Planning "Essential Projects" that excite and inspire you.

- Establishing "Essential Connections" by keeping in touch with your favorite people.

As you get the hang of it, you'll find yourself living "Essential Days," where even the busiest moments reflect what truly matters to you.

A Bite-Size Challenge

Ditty Ditching is about saying "no" to unnecessary things so we can create space to say "yes" to what truly matters to us. For the next week, practice saying "yes" to small things that are important to you. It could be:

→ Taking a 10-minute walk outside to enjoy nature.

→ Spending a few minutes each day reading a book you love.

→ Setting aside time for a hobby that brings you joy.

→ Calling or texting a friend who lifts your spirits.

→ Enjoying a favorite treat without guilt.

Celebrate each "yes" and notice how it adds more joy and fulfillment to your days.[*]

Step 4: Make Every Decision an Essential One

Having clarity about what's important to you is like having a personal Rosetta Stone for deciphering the Ditties, Deeds, Duties, and Delights in your life. This discernment becomes a guiding

---

*Special thank you to our colleague Dr. Maria Sirois, who inspired this Bite-Size Challenge by once asking us the profound question: "How are you saying 'yes' in small ways?"

compass when making decisions about what to say "yes" and "no" to. When you're clear on your Essentials, that all-important foundational Ditty-Ditching question— *"Is this something I want to do?"*—becomes much easier to answer.

Using the ABCDE Essentials as a framework can help serve as a litmus test whenever new asks come your way. Next time you're trying to decide *"Is this something I want to do?"* consider also asking yourself:

Achievements:

- Does this opportunity align with my long-term goals and ambitions?

- Will saying "yes" help me progress toward my desired achievements?

- How does this align with my vision of success and personal growth?

Belongings:

- Does saying "yes" support my ability to provide for myself?

- Will saying "yes" contribute positively to my physical living environment?

Characteristics:

- Does saying "yes" resonate with my core values and beliefs?

- Will this decision reflect positively on my character and integrity?

- How does this align with the person I strive to be and the qualities I want to embody?

Darlings:

- How will saying "yes" impact my relationships with loved ones?

- Will this decision strengthen or strain my important connections?

Experiences:

- Will this opportunity result in a memory I'll look back on fondly?

- Does this align with my intention to seek meaningful experiences?

If you look more closely at the Ditty Decision Tree, you'll find that only 25% of it is about saying "no" and 75% is about saying "yes" with clear intentions. Learning to Ditch Ditties is just as much about gaining the confidence to say "yes" to those things that bring us joy as it is about saying "no" to the things that don't. It also helps us become better decision-makers, manage unnecessary stress, avoid burnout, and, ultimately, be more present for what matters most to us.

So, we invite you to put your Essentials to work for you. Use them as a lens through which you look at opportunities and decide what action best aligns with what truly matters to you, ensuring that your energy and time are invested in pursuits that bring you fulfillment and joy. This clarity empowers you to confidently decline opportunities or commitments that don't align with your values or goals, freeing up space for activities and relationships that nourish you. For example, perhaps you don't really need to plan the office party for the fifth time or organize the family reunion, including coordinating schedules and dietary preferences for relatives near and far!

By understanding your Essentials, you can discern when to gracefully decline invitations or requests that may distract you from your goals or drain your resources. Saying "no" to Ditties is a form of self-care and self-respect that not only preserves your sanity but also sends a message to the universe that your needs matter, too. And conversely, when you can confidently embrace the right opportunities, it's like giving life a big high-five. You're curating your own authentic adventure, one enthusiastic "Heck YES!" at a time.

Ditty Decision Tree

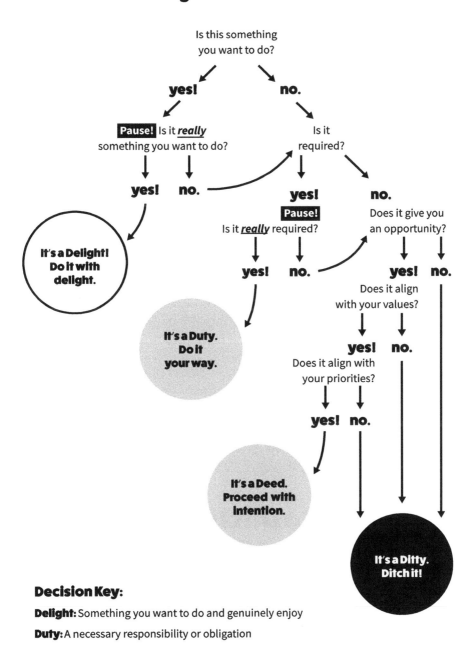

Decision Key:

Delight: Something you want to do and genuinely enjoy

Duty: A necessary responsibility or obligation

Deed: An unwanted task that offers other opportunities

Ditty: Something you neither want nor need to do

Step 5: Evolve Your Essentials As Needed

There's another secret we want to let you in on as you work on crafting your Essential-filled life:

You can change your mind.

You're not affirming your eternal membership in the *"Stuck-With-This Society"* when you identify what matters to you. These things can—and likely will—change as your life unfolds. Yep! Your Essentials can evolve!

As we were reflecting on the topic of Essentials, a headline appeared that stopped us in our tracks. There, among the daily news of messy politics and ongoing global turmoil, we learned that Marie Kondo said she was moving on from tidying.[109]

What?!? Wasn't tidying her "thing"? She'd built an entire empire on being known as a "professional tidier" and then she said, "My home is messy, but the way I am spending my time is the right way for me at this time, at this stage of my life."[110] After getting over the initial shock of this news, we decided perhaps we needed to take a page from Marie's playbook, and we began asking ourselves:

Is it time to Ditch yesterday's Essentials if they no longer fit us today?

What we realized in our exploration of our Essentials is that they're not fixed, nor do they need to be. As our lives evolve, so do our priorities, including what—and even whom—we hold dear. For women especially, navigating the different stages of life brings about shifts in perspective and values. What may have been cru-

THE ULTIMATE QUESTION: WHAT DO YOU REALLY WANT?

cial in our 20s might take a backseat in our 30s and completely transform by our 40s—then again in our 50s, 60s, and beyond. Influenced by experiences, responsibilities, and personal growth, your answer to "What matters most?" will evolve, just as you do, across your life.

Even if Marie is no longer focusing on tidying like she once was, we still find inspiration in the idea of our lives being a bit like a "Kondo closet" that needs to be sorted from time to time. At different stages, you'll rummage through the shelves, discovering items that once held great significance but now gather dust in the shadows. As you sift through the clutter, you may stumble upon treasures you never knew existed or find that certain outfits no longer fit you.

Just as you periodically clean out your wardrobe, getting rid of items that no longer serve you and embracing new pieces that fit your evolving style, your perception of what matters most also undergoes constant refinement. Over time, you may find yourself rearranging the contents of your mental closet, swapping out outdated goals and aspirations for fresh ones that better reflect your current desires and circumstances. This ongoing process of introspection and reevaluation allows you to curate a collection of priorities that truly align with and fit who you are and where you're headed at each stage of life.

After a recent conversation with one of us, our colleague Anita beautifully expressed the importance of recognizing what we might want to let go:

> "When we were talking yesterday, I mentioned how I wanted to be on a board. The next morning, I was kind of beating myself up that I had not moved on that goal. Getting things done is one of my superpowers. Then I had my aha moment—I don't want that anymore—it's a dragged along, "expired" goal. It is important to learn how to listen to the soul-messages bundled in the emotions of procrastination and dread."

Anita's insight around releasing "expired" goals reminded us of the wisdom of management guru Peter Drucker, who introduced the concept of "purposeful abandonment" as an important strate-gy for successful organizations. He wrote:

> "Planned, purposeful abandonment of the old and of the unrewarding is a prerequisite to successful pursuit of the new and highly promising. Above all, abandonment is the key to innovation—both because it frees the neces-sary resources and because it stimulates the search for the new that will replace the old."[111]

Drucker's idea of purposeful abandonment (what a great phrase!) isn't just for businesses; it's a game changer for our personal lives, too. Letting go of outdated goals and unnecessary commitments frees up our time and energy for the things that truly light us up, making life more fulfilling and Delight-*full*.

A Bite-Size Challenge

We invite you to play with the notion of purposeful aban-donment and allow yourself to have a "Goal Memorial Ser-vice." Take a moment to reflect on an unachieved goal in your life that you no longer want to pursue. Write a short eulogy for this goal, acknowledging the effort you put into it and the lessons you learned. Consider what new goals or directions have emerged as a result of letting this expired goal go. Finally, say a few words of farewell to honor its place in your journey.

While any time may be good for an Essentials reevaluation, we've put together 10 particularly apropos moments to check in about what matters in our lives. These include:

1. Milestone birthdays (e.g., turning 30, 40, 50, 60…)

2. After significant life events, like marriage or divorce

3. After having children or becoming an empty nester

4. After achieving a long-term goal or accomplishment

5. Dealing with a health scare or illness— for yourself or a loved one

6. In the wake of experiencing loss or grief

7. When experiencing a financial windfall or setback

8. When entering a new professional phase, such as a new job or retirement

9. Following periods of intense stress or burnout

10. When you wake up with your mind spinning at 2:14 am

Regardless of the reason, don't be afraid to continually explore your metaphorical life closet and Ditch those Essentials that no longer fit you. We don't need to be defined by what we did last year, last week, yesterday, or even five minutes ago. From considering career changes to relationship evolutions or mindset shifts (for us this includes reconsidering our "polite perfectionism" and our "fix-it-for-everyone-fastidiousness"), there are always things that we may need to let go of from yesterday to become who we want to be today.

After all, if Marie Kondo can release herself from an endless tidying quest, can't we give up some of those things that we have long used to identify ourselves but that no longer make us happy?

Part 4 Ditty-Ditching Duhs

Answering the question "What do you want?" is crucial for being able to Ditch Ditties. The answer may not be immediately clear—and it may evolve over time. Here are some Ditty Duhs to help you continue clarifying your answer to that critical question.

1. **W-A-N-T is Not a Four-Letter Word:** Okay, technically it is a four-letter word, but it's not a dirty word. We spend so much energy as women tending to everyone else's wants that giving time and space to our own needs can feel a bit funky at first. It's like trying on a new pair of shoes—a little awkward at the start, but the more you walk around in them, the more comfortable they feel.

2. **The Importance of Learning Your ABCDEs:** Understanding your Essential ABCDEs (Achievements, Belongings, Characteristics, Darlings, and Experiences) is crucial for figuring out the Essentials you truly want to carry. By identifying what matters most, you can prioritize your time and energy, Ditch unnecessary Ditties, and focus on the things that bring you genuine fulfillment and joy.

3. **One Size Does Not Need to Fit Forever:** Just as our wardrobe changes with the seasons, so too do our Essentials and priorities. What we feel comfortable with one day may not be the same the next. Reflecting on the Essentials that fit us is a lifelong journey.

4. **Essentials Help Us Say "No" AND "Yes" More Confidently:** Ditching Ditties is about gaining clarity on both our "nos" and our "yeses." By spending time identifying what is truly essential for yourself, you can navigate the Ditty Decision Tree with both speed and confidence, resulting in actions that help you live your life more authentically.

PART 5
The Dynamics of Ditching & Scaling Your "No"

You've come a long way! By now, you:

☑ Know what a Ditty is and isn't.

☑ Recognize the importance of Ditching Ditties in your life.

☑ Are familiar with the Ditty Dynamics that color your awareness and acceptance of Ditties.

☑ Can unmask some of the most common Ditty Disguises.

☑ Understand why the question "What do you want?" can be so tricky to answer.

☑ Have a deeper awareness of the ABCDEs that matter most to you.

Don't you wish there was a badge for each of these skills that you could add to your resume or LinkedIn profile? Go ahead and add them. We'll back you up!

There's still one crucial skill that we need to explore in our journey to becoming the Ditty-Ditching divas that we all aspire to be. You've probably guessed it. We're reaching the peak of our Ditty-Ditching journey—and therefore we must master the art of delivering and scaling our "no." It's a challenging climb, but trust us, the view from the top is worth it. So, grab those oxygen masks again and let's tackle this final peak together! To begin, let's recognize that:

Sorry is NOT the hardest word.

No offense to Sir Elton John, but we think he got it wrong with his song title "Sorry Seems to Be the Hardest Word."[112] For us, "sorry" seems to roll off our tongues all day long. It's another word that we find more challenging to say: "NO."

For women, the art of saying "no" without guilt often seems as elusive as uncovering a genuine diamond in a sea of zirconia. From our earliest encounters with this word, we're conditioned to view it as a blasphemous syllable we're not supposed to utter. After all, isn't it our job to prioritize others' happiness and needs all the time? Saying "yes" to others' asks and tasks often feels like the path of least resistance toward that goal.

So, before we delve into strategies for gracefully declining without feeling buried in guilt or facing an avalanche of pushback, let's examine another set of dynamics that influence our ability to utter that all-important "no." Reflecting yet again on the realities of gendered socialization we began discussing in Part 2, it's no surprise that "no" remains one of our hardest words to say. The same messages we internalize about being nice, polite, and helpful cloud not only our ability to recognize Ditties but also our comfort with Ditching them. Whereas the Ditty Dynamics we explored in Part 2 help us understand the former tendency, we also posit that there are Ditching Dynamics that creep up and impact the latter.

Specifically, we define this as:

Ditching Dynamic

/'diCHiNG/ /dī'namik/ *noun*

1. an internalized gender socialization that affects how we say "no" to unwanted and unnecessary requests
2. a socialized habit of feeling angst when saying "no" to requests

Once again, integrating existing research, our conversations with women, and our own lived experiences, we've found that the three most common Ditching Dynamics are:

1. **The Apologetic Angel**

2. **The Ruminating Ruby**

3. **The Magic Wand**

Let's look at each of these dynamics in turn to better understand why those two little letters "N" and "O" can be so elusive some-times—even when we know we want to deliver them.

Ditching Dynamic: The Apologetic Angel

This Ditching Dynamic explores the tendency for women to use the word "sorry" more frequently than necessary, particularly when declining a request. Regardless of what Elton sings, "sorry" does in fact seem to be an easy word for women to say.

Research shows that:

- Women apologize more often than men.[113]

- Women comprise over 75% of the total observed reported apologies in certain situations.[114]

- Women have a lower threshold than men for what they consider offensive.[115]

This data echoed our own pesky penchant for apologizing to everyone and everything in our lives. For example, we laughed over the following all-true experience.

The Ditty Diaries: Miriam's Story

I was strolling through the grocery store aisles, trying to get everything on my list before the after-work crowd hit. I was grabbing a bunch of bananas when, suddenly, another shopper's cart came barreling around the corner and crashed into my parked cart.

"Oh, I'm so sorry!" I exclaimed instinctively, even though it was clearly the other person's fault. She hadn't been looking where she was going at all. I laughed to distract from the awkwardness of the moment, noticing a few items had fallen out of my cart. The other person replied, "No worries at all," and continued on their way as I bent down to pick up my items.

It wasn't until the checkout line that I realized I had apologized to someone who'd bumped into me!

We also each have our own stories of the many times we've written email responses with classic openers such as:

- *"I am sorry it has taken me a while to get back to you…"*

- *"Sorry to bother you, but…"*

- *"So sorry to have missed your call…"*

- *"I'm sorry, I need a little more time to get that information…"*

You likely have your own anthology of apologetic openers for emails, phone calls, meetings, grocery store run-ins…you name it! As women, the apologies seem to just exponentially soar when we're working to deliver a "no" to someone.

We understand the emotional ribbons that so often wrap themselves around the word "no": fear, anxiety, sadness, discomfort, hesitation. Especially given our socialization as women to accommodate and please others, the idea of simply saying "no" can feel paralyzing. As a result, we package our "nos" in bubble wrap to help ensure a softer delivery for the recipient. We apologize and explain why we have to say "no" as if it's something beyond our control. This pattern is so ingrained, we almost have a blueprint for our negative replies that goes something like:

> **Step 1: The Apology.** We make sure they know how very sorry we are that we can't accommodate their request. We say, "I'm so sorry…"
>
> **Step 2: The Justification.** We make sure they know that of course we would've replied with an affirmative if only we weren't already committed to something very worthwhile and thus physically or temporarily unable to accommodate their request. We say, "I can't come to your meeting because I'm already committed to deworming kittens at the local animal shelter or _____ [add in something worthwhile you're already committed to] that same afternoon."
>
> **Step 3: The Alternative.** We make sure they know we're still a nice person by suggesting a substitute solution or offering to somehow make it up to them. We say, "Even though I can't come at that time, I'd be glad to meet with you another time or help out in some other way."
>
> **Step 4: The Bookend Apology.** We apologize again to make sure they remember we're nice and don't think badly of us. We say, "Again, I'm so sorry I can't come."

We refer to this tendency to "beg-your-pardon" with every person who crosses our path or every negative reply we need to deliver as The Apologetic Angel.

The Apologetic Angel

/əˌpäləˈjedik/ /ˈānjəl/ *proper noun*
>   One who offers apologies when she has nothing to apologize for. "I'm sorry" is her go-to balm for any real or perceived awkwardness or tension while aiming to keep peace and ensure everyone's comfortable.

This dynamic is so prevalent that someone has even developed an app called "Just Not Sorry" to help women stop writing "sorry" in their emails.[116] This tool is used to scan emails, highlighting where extraneous instances of "just" and "sorry" are included in the message, suggesting alternative phrases instead. If only we had a similar app for our brains to help us circumvent those unnecessary apologies before they even form. We imagine it would be akin to the *South Park* movie where Cartman was fitted with a v-chip that shocked him every time he cussed to help break his profanity habit.[117]

We recognize that there are many times in our lives when an apology is warranted, and there are many social benefits for both the giver and receiver of a sincere "I'm sorry." The ability to apologize has been associated with healthy child development, signaling the emergence of empathy and social skills. As we mature in our relational skills, authentic apologies have been shown to help mend relationships, build emotional connections, and serve as a deterrent for future offenses.[118] But we're not talking about those moments where a true transgression has occurred, and a mindful apology is warranted. Rather, we're talking about our knee-jerk habitual response as women to belt out an "I'm sorry" as the opening stanza of any song we're singing.

Understanding where our susceptibility for saying "I'm sorry" comes from can help us become more intentional in our apologies. Dr. Maja Jovanic, a sociology professor and author of *Hey Ladies, Stop Apologizing…And Other Career Mistakes Women Make*, suggests that our tendency for apologies is rooted in our fear of not being liked.[119] This aligns with The Persistent Pleaser research we discussed earlier. Similarly, Dr. Stephen Hinshaw, clinical psychologist and author of *The Triple Bind: Saving Our Teenage Girls from Today's Pressures and Conflicting Expectations*, emphasizes how more so than boys, girls receive messages to be empathetic, making them hyper-aware of how their actions affect others.[120] For instance, while a boy might win a race without considering its impact on competitors, a girl may downplay her success out of concern for others' feelings.[121]

Think this is just an abstract anecdote? Consider the real-life story from the 2018 U.S. Open championship, when Naomi Osaka apologized for winning against fan-favorite Serena Williams.[122] As Osaka reflected in an interview on the *Today Show* after her win, "I just felt like everyone was sort of unhappy up there. I just felt very emotional, and I felt that I had to apologize."[123] So, she apologized…for winning the U.S. Open.

For us, the question is:

When should we perhaps be #SorryNotSorry?

When we mindlessly dish out apologies, they can become meaningless and undermine the messages that we're trying to convey that follow the apology. As neuroscientist and author Dr. Tara Swart reflects, serial apologists mostly do so out of habit, perhaps stemming from a childhood where they were made to feel wrong or fearful of punishment. She notes that "Apologizing when we have done something wrong is a real strength, but compulsive apologizing presents as a weakness at work and in personal relationships."[124]

You might ask yourself, "How do I know if I'm overly apologizing?" Our top 10 signs that you might be an overly Apologetic Angel include:

1. Your ringtone is Nirvana's "All Apologies."[125]

2. Your daily "I'm sorry" count exceeds your daily step count.

3. You've said "sorry" on a Zoom call before you've even said "Hello."

4. You apologize to inanimate objects when you bump into them.

5. You apologize when your stomach growls, as if you can control it.

6. You apologize to the waiter when your food comes out wrong.

7. You know how to say "I'm sorry" in more than one language.

8. You apologize even when you're right in an argument.

9. You say "sorry" when someone else interrupts *you* during a conversation.

10. You apologize for apologizing too much.

How many of these signs resonate with you? How many times have you said "I'm sorry" this week…today…in the last five minutes? If you're anything like us, you may feel like you're a character in the hilarious-yet-all-too-true "I'm Sorry" sketch from the show *Inside Amy Schumer.* In the scene, the women find themselves apologizing for everything…from others mispronouncing their name to someone spilling hot coffee on them.[126] (And if you haven't seen this skit, give yourself the three-minute gift of watching it!) We love that in real life, Amy has said she's learned "Not to apologize before putting my two cents in. I noticed I was starting my sentences with 'sorry' and [when] I cut that out, I left the set feeling very empowered."[127]

If we feel that every "no" must be wrapped in an "I'm sorry," we add extra emotional weight to saying "no" and may end up saying "yes" to any request or task. By Ditching the unnecessary apologies, we can say "no" more confidently and preserve our energy for the things that really matter.

As always, awareness is our friend here. Simply becoming more aware of our habit of feeling the need to apologize constantly is crucial for making intentional decisions and mastering the art of Ditching Ditties.

A Bite-Size Challenge

As you work to silence the habitual apologies when declining a Ditty, ask yourself:

→ How can I say "no" without wrapping it in an apologetic bow?

→ If I imagined that I had a limited supply of "sorry sauce" to spread across my life, is this a situation that truly warrants the distribution of an apology?

→ What message do I want to convey, and does saying "sorry" align with that message or dilute it?

Ditching Dynamic: The Ruminating Ruby

This Ditching Dynamic dives into the tendency of women to get our mental frequencies stuck on the rumination radio station when we're faced with delivering a "no" to someone. Rumination is like having a song stuck in your head, but instead of music, it's the same worry or concern playing on repeat over and over. The reverberating notes of overthinking and second-guessing ourselves that come with rumination can make it tricky for us to confidently assert ourselves and say "no" even when we want to.

Research shows that:

- Women are more likely than men to ruminate around stressful events, and this gender difference is even more pronounced for interpersonal events.[128]

- Gender differences in rumination appear in adolescence and remain into adulthood.[129]

- Women consistently report higher rates of depression, anxiety, and other conditions associated with ruminative strategies.[130]

We have so many stories of getting ourselves stuck on the rumination station. Here's just one of them.

The Ditty Diary: Molly's Story

I recently found myself faced with a tempting collaboration opportunity with a colleague. Despite its allure, I took the time to work through my Ditty Decision Tree and ultimately decided that the opportunity wasn't the right fit for me at that time. I thoughtfully and respectfully declined via email, leaving the door open for future collaboration.

As the days passed without a response from my colleague, my mind began to spin with negative assumptions. I bet you can hear the soundtrack that looped through my mind, with those reverberating familiar notes:

- ♫ *He is mad at me.*

- ♫ *He is really mad at me.*

- ♫ *He thinks I blew him off and is disappointed.*

- ♫ *He thinks I'm not worthy of a response.*

- ♫ *He will never reach out to me again.*

- ♫ *No one will ever ask me to do anything again; my career is over. La, la la!*

As those notes played over and over again in my head, it never occurred to me to push the pause button and imagine that there might be reasons for his silence that had nothing to do with me. Finally, a week later, his reply arrived, filled with warmth and understanding. He apologized for the delay (yes, he apologized!), explaining that a family crisis had demanded his attention, thus delaying his email replies. He went on to share how much he'd love to connect to think about future partnerships.

After receiving his email, I realized how much time I had wasted stewing and worrying for nothing. While I wished those negative thoughts were a one-hit wonder never to return, I knew they were in my Billboard Top 10 hits of all time and would likely pop back up again the next time I had to decline someone else's ask.

Changing the channel to our personal lives, here is another example of how this tendency shows up.

The Ditty Diary: Lindsey's Story

To be completely honest, I get a jingle bell-sized pit in my stomach every time the holidays roll around, knowing I'm about to be overwhelmed by invitations to holiday get-togethers. With every evite, text, and embossed invitation that shows up on my doorstep, my mind races with the possible consequences of saying "no" to the 10th "ugly sweater party" I just don't want to attend. I fret, telling myself, "If I decline, they'll think I don't care and I might never be invited again" and picturing my friends worrying over why I don't want to come.

Over time, however, I've learned that I need quiet evenings to recharge, especially during the holidays. So, I've been practicing taking deep breaths and politely declining gatherings I just can't handle. Guess what? I've discovered that my friends don't see me as the Grinch for saying "no." Just like Dr. Seuss's Whos in Whoville remind us that the holidays can come "without packages, boxes, or bags,"[131] I've realized they can also come without me attending every event in December.

You, too, could probably fill an entire double album with tracks from your own rumination station. We refer to the tendency for us to overthink, then overthink overthinking, as "The Ruminating Ruby."

The Ruminating Ruby

/rῡoməˌnāt ing/ /ˈrῡobē/ *proper noun*
> One who endlessly overthinks her responses, always worrying about how others will react. This habit often leads to needless stress and turns both past and anticipated conversations into mental marathons.

It's perhaps no surprise that as women our brains have a built-in DJ playing a never-ending loop of that ever-catchy song *"Why did they look at me that way?"* followed by an encore of *"What will they think of me if I do that?"* These songs are well-ingrained from a young age, thanks again to those expectations and gender norms that emphasize women should be empathetic and nurturing. Consequently, we have an increased sensitivity to how our actions and words are perceived by others. This results in us often second-guessing ourselves and worrying about what everyone else thinks with each message we deliver.

While this news isn't new, what's interesting is that one of our favorite coping mechanisms as women may actually exacerbate this dynamic. What might that be? Co-ruminating with others! That's right...rehashing our ruminations with our girlfriends can result in increased angst and even more worry. Co-ruminating is defined as "Excessively talking with another person about problems, including rehashing them and dwelling on the negative feelings associated with them."[132] And it has been shown to have both pros and cons for those of us stuck on thinking about a situation. Research has shown that, specifically for girls, co-rumination has a positive effect on friendship quality, including feelings of closeness between friends, but it's also associated with an increase in feelings of anxiety.[133] These feelings then contribute to greater co-rumination.

And round and round we go!

We share all this not to prevent that ever-helpful commiserating that we all enjoy from time to time—as these moments do help strengthen our bonds of friendship. Rather, we simply want to raise awareness of the fact that co-rumination can sometimes exacerbate worry and angst rather than alleviate it. While sharing our concerns and seeking support from friends is a natural inclination, dwelling excessively on problems together can inadvertently amplify negative emotions. As we exchange stories and analyze situations, we may find ourselves caught in a cycle of rumination, each adding fuel to the other's worries. Instead of offering constructive solutions or a fresh perspective, co-ruminating can reinforce negative thought patterns and intensify feelings of distress. It's important to strike a balance between venting with friends and actively seeking solutions, recognizing when co-ruminating may be perpetuating rather than alleviating our concerns.

For us, the question is:

When should we change the channel on the Rumination Station?

As women, we often get trapped in overthinking mode, especially when faced with the daunting task of saying "no" to someone. This endless rumination can lead to a vicious cycle of doubt, anxiety, and self-criticism. (Cue The Persistent Pleaser, The Perfect Pearl, and The Self-Doubting Dame!) Breaking free from this mental loop is crucial because it allows us to gain clarity and perspective on the situation and deliver our "nos" without that unwanted internalized guilt. Recognizing when our thoughts are veering into a negative spiral empowers us to take proactive steps, like seeking support from friends (without turning it into a worry-fest), practicing self-compassion, or engaging in activities that distract us from rumination. Ultimately, interrupting rumination helps you make decisions that align with your true desires and values—perhaps it would be helpful to refer back to your Essentials work from Part 4—rather than being swayed by your projection of others' expectations.

You might ask yourself, "How do I know if I'm over-ruminating?" Our top 10 signs that you might be stuck at the Rumination Station include:

1. Your bedtime routine includes a mental marathon of replaying every awkward moment from the day.

2. You've mentally replayed a conversation with your boss from three weeks ago at least 10 times.

3. You've spent more time thinking about your past mistakes than planning your next vacation.

4. Your brain is always writing a new chapter in your "worst-case scenario" handbook.

5. Your friends can recite your worries verbatim because they've heard them so many times.

6. You've lost sleep over something that happened over a year ago.

7. You've spent days mentally rewriting an email you already sent, debating whether you need to send a follow-up with an addendum.

8. You've analyzed a casual text message from a friend for hidden meanings.

9. Your inner critic has a megaphone, and it's constantly yelling, "You messed up!"

10. You've turned "what ifs" into an Olympic sport, and you're going for the gold in catastrophizing.

Again, awareness is our friend. Acknowledging our tendency to ruminate is like finding the remote control for that stuck channel and finally flipping to a new station that's playing a much better tune.

A Bite-Size Challenge

When you're faced with delivering a "no" that's sending you into a Ruminating Ruby loop, ask yourself:

→ If this situation was an episode of a true crime show, what evidence would I have that what I'm worrying about is really true?

→ Is my imagination trying to win an award for best dramatic screenplay in this situation?

→ What other stories might be true regarding someone's response to my "no" that have nothing to do with me?

Mental Health Note on Rumination

While we're diving into the topic of rumination, it's important to note that some of what we're describing here are intrusive thoughts. These could be symptoms of anxiety, post-traumatic stress disorders, or other conditions[134] and not just a by-product of how women are socialized. If rumination is preventing you from functioning in your daily actions, you may want to seek support. Taking care of your mental health is paramount, and there's no shame in reaching out for help.

Ditching Dynamic: The Magic Wand

This Ditching Dynamic explores the tendency of women to feel responsible for still magically finding a solution, even when we say "no" to someone's request.

See if this scene feels vaguely familiar:

A friend comes to you in a full-blown panic, desperately seeking your help with a massive event they're planning. As they lay out their problem, you're all ears, fully engaged, and ready to offer support. But then comes the kicker: You realize you can't be the one to save the day. Maybe you're swamped with your own commitments and literally do not have time to assist with their grand plans or perhaps the logistics are simply beyond your skill set (hard to imagine, we know!). Despite clearly knowing you have to say "no" to their plea for help, you feel a relentless, almost heroic urge to find someone else who can rescue them. It's like you're on a mission from the universe, scouring your mental Rolodex for potential saviors to their challenge, determined to ensure that even if you can't be the superhero in this story, you'll assemble an entire team of Avengers to step up to the plate. In this case, saying "no" doesn't mean the end of the road for you—it just means orchestrating an elaborate rescue operation to help them out, even if you're not leading the charge.

Let's dive into some more data:

- Research suggests that compared to men, women exhibit higher levels of prosocial behavior, including acts of assistance, sharing, and providing comfort to others.[135]

- Studies have demonstrated that women, even those who embrace traditionally masculine qualities such as power, dominance, and independence, display higher levels of altruism than men.[136]

- At a neurological level, it has been demonstrated that women's brains show increased activation in response to acts of prosocial behavior, while men's brains exhibit greater activation when engaged in selfish behavior.[137]

This is a tale we've lived many times, as these two stories illustrate:

The Ditty Diaries: Lindsey's Story

I was leading the planning for a professional conference, complete with overseeing the review process for speakers. As a flood of submissions inundated my inbox, I found myself in a bind: There were too many proposals and not enough slots on the agenda. Torn between the need to reject numerous deserving applicants and my aversion to delivering bad news to anyone, I embarked on a quest to find a solution.

Instead of mustering the courage to simply say "no" to the excess submissions, I concocted a last-minute addition to the program where the rejected presenters could still showcase their work via pre-recorded presentations that others could watch on demand. While this gesture may have appeased the disappointed applicants, it only added to my already overwhelming workload. Thus, with each additional presenter accommodated, I found myself sinking deeper into a quagmire of logistical nightmares and stress, all because I couldn't bring myself to utter that dreaded two-letter word without also providing a helpful pathway to soften the blow of the "no."

The Ditty Diaries: Andi's Story

When I was in my 20s and in grad school, my best friend, Jenna, called me in a panic one Friday afternoon. She had a big work event that weekend and had just found out that her babysitter canceled last minute. She knew I had plans to study for a major exam—and didn't really like babies— but she was desperate for help with her three-month-old. Despite knowing how important it was for me to focus on my studies, I couldn't quite bring myself to say "no" to her.

Instead of babysitting, I decided to find her a replacement. "Don't worry, Jenna. I'll find someone to watch the baby," I assured her. I then spent the next three hours

*calling everyone I knew and even knocking on neighbors'
doors. It felt like a wild goose chase, and with each passing minute, I realized how much easier it would have been
just to babysit myself.*

*Finally, after what felt like an eternity, I found a friend of
a friend who could step in. I called Jenna with the good
news, and she was incredibly relieved. While she thanked
me profusely, I couldn't shake the feeling that I'd wasted
precious hours that could have been spent studying. My
head was spinning from the effort, and my study schedule
was completely thrown off.*

*Even though I managed to help Jenna without directly
babysitting, the whole ordeal left me exhausted and frus-
trated. I realized that sometimes, in my effort to help, I
end up creating more work and stress for myself.*

You likely have your own stories of going above and beyond to
"fix it" even when you had to decline an ask. We refer to the tendency to give others hope, even when we have to say "nope," as
The Magic Wand.

The Magic Wand

/majik/ /wand/ *proper noun*
    One who always tries to conjure up solutions for
    others, even when saying "no" to their requests.
    She's constantly waving her wand to "fix it" for ev-
    eryone, even when it's not her problem to solve.

Reflecting on the research, it's perhaps no surprise that we have
a litany of stories about how we've tried to be a fairy godmother,
still granting wishes even when we're saying "no." Our brains lit-

erally crave the feel-good sensation that comes from helping others. When we unfurl our magical wings to help someone out, our brains light up with what has been referred to as the "happiness trifecta" of neurochemicals, otherwise known as serotonin (the bliss booster), dopamine (the energy elixir) and oxytocin (the relational rocket fuel).[138] So of course we like helping others; it can feel like getting a happy hour in our heads, minus the hangover!

Before we jump on the "nature" side of the nature-nurture debate about gender differences, it's important to recognize the interplay between nature and nurture that impacts our gendered brain development. While research has found that women's brains literally react more strongly to prosocial behaviors than men's brains, neuroscientists have warned against overly confounding correlation and causation. Dr. Alexander Soutschek from the University of Zurich reminds us that the reward and learning areas of our brain are perhaps more intertwined than we realize. He summarizes:

> *"Empirical studies show that girls are rewarded with praise for prosocial behavior, implying that their reward systems learn to expect a reward for helping behavior instead of selfish behavior. With this in mind, the gender differences that we observed in our studies could be attributed to the different cultural expectations placed on men and women."[139]*

Perhaps nurture impacts our nature. Either way, women often feel the pressure to swoop in and grant *bonus* wishes even when we know we've got to drop the "no" bomb. It's like we want to have our cake and eat it, too, thinking we can say "no" AND still save the day. Years of conditioning tell us that we should be the caregivers, the fixers, the everything-to-everyone folks. So, even when we decline, we still scramble to find a way to sprinkle some magic dust on the problem and make it all better—because saying "no" just doesn't feel right without at least trying to be the fairy godmother in the background. Sometimes, however, our quest to perpeually deliver fairy dust to others leaves us feeling famished instead of refueled.

For us, the question is:

When does our quest to help others hurt us?

While wanting to help others can create many positive outcomes—from our own feeling of euphoria thanks to those "happy hormones" our brains release, to strengthening social bonds with others—there can also be a limit to the benefits. At a certain point, we can become so focused on saving the day that it can become a preoccupation that turns helping into an Achilles' heel. Clinical psychologists Drs. Mary Lamia and Marilyn Krieger, authors of *The White Knight Syndrome: Rescuing Yourself from Your Need to Rescue Others*, suggest that sometimes we may become compulsive rescuers, basing our self-worth on our ability to fix others.[140] In these extreme cases, we like donning our magic tiara, but it's more about enjoying how we look in that jeweled crown than it is for actually helping others.

If you genuinely enjoy how you look in the tiara, great! The issue arises when rescuing becomes a compulsion driven by the need for validation rather than a genuine wish to assist. Recognize when helping others starts to compromise your well-being and find a balance that allows you to contribute without losing yourself. Otherwise, you risk always promising to grant others' wishes even when you want to be delivering "nos," leaving yourself drained and exhausted. This pattern can take a toll on your mental and physical health, leading to resentment and frustration. Research shows that when you constantly prioritize others' needs over your own, your determination to pursue your own goals may diminish, leaving you with little energy to help yourself.[141]

Don't get us wrong, helping others is admirable and something we strive for. We're talking about the over-the-top, constant wand waving and wish granting that leaves us feeling like we need our own Fairy Godmother—except this one hands out naps and "no" buttons instead of glass slippers. Unsure if your helpfulness is tipping into overdrive? Here are our top 10 signs:

1. You find yourself saying, "I'll do it!" before anyone else has a chance to blink.

2. Your phone's contact list is filled with people who only call when they need something, and you're always there to answer.

3. You're the unofficial office therapist, constantly lending an ear and offering advice to colleagues, even during your lunch break.

4. Your calendar looks like a game of Tetris, filled with back-to-back commitments to help friends, family, and neighbors.

5. Your idea of relaxation involves running errands for friends or volunteering for yet another committee.

6. You've got a reputation as the neighborhood fixer-upper, always on call for home repairs or tech support, even for things you don't know how to do.

7. You've offered to dog-sit, even though you're allergic to dogs.

8. You feel a sense of obligation to solve everyone's problems, even when they haven't asked for your help.

9. Your personal motto is "help now, sleep later."

10. You feel like a human Swiss Army knife—always equipped to solve any problem, which has left you feeling a bit dull around the edges.

Recognizing excessive wand waving is crucial for safeguarding your time and energy. By acknowledging these signs, you can strike a better balance between supporting others and maintaining your well-being. Remember saying "no" doesn't always require a further solution.

A Bite-Size Challenge

The next time you need to say "no" but still feel the urge to whip out your magic wand, ask yourself:

→ Am I slipping into Fairy Godmother mode, trying to grant wishes even after I've already said "no?"

→ What would it look like if I turned my helping tendency inward and helped myself by NOT doing anything other than declining this request?

→ Would I still expect assistance from others if they declined my request in a similar situation?

Armed with an understanding of these three Ditching Dynamics, you're geared up with your hiking essentials and ready to conquer the final peak in your Ditching journey: mastering the skill of saying "no."

Saying "Yes" to Saying "No"

That magical word.

No.

There's so much power in it; it can create an earthquake of impact. Perhaps that's why we're hesitant to wield it. We're afraid of the aftershocks that will ripple through our lives when we dare to utter it. Yet, when we learn to use it effectively, this little word can have a seismic impact on de-Dittying our lives.

"No" isn't a bad word. As we have explored, it also doesn't need to cozy up next to a bunch of other words of apology or justification to make its point—it's perfectly capable of standing on its own two feet. "No" is, in fact, a complete sentence. Wait…that's an important point. Let's repeat it louder:

"No" is a complete sentence.[142]

Repeat that mantra to yourself a few times. Got it? Okay, now simply hold this two-letter word in your mind. Say it to yourself in different tones: hesitant, determined, defiant, amused, confident.

No.

No.

No.

No.

Now say it out loud. Do it alone if you want, or if you want to have some fun, just start saying it wherever you're reading this—especially if that's in line at the coffee shop and they just asked if you want to try the strange flavor of the month instead of your beloved usual order.

No.

No.

No.

No.

Easy, right? Yeah, easy like skydiving. In theory, when we're safe on the ground, thinking about jumping out of a plane seems like an uncomplicated feat: you just take a little step and jump, easy-peasy. In reality, when you're soaring 15,000 feet above the ground with wind whipping around your head and your stomach in your throat, jumping seems a lot more complicated. Similarly, the simple act of saying "no" in real life can feel like you're free-falling, sometimes without a parachute.

Scaling Your "No"

Just as all asks aren't created equal, not all "nos" need to be delivered in the same way. Some may need to come out as firm and resolute as a steel door slamming shut, while others can be delivered with a softer touch. The way we deliver our "no" can vary depending on the situation, the person we're speaking to, and our own comfort level with the dynamics we've already explored. But regardless of how it's delivered, every "no" deserves to be respected and honored—whether you're saying "no" like a mic drop or whispering it like a secret.

We'd never ask you to do something that the three of us haven't tried. As such, we've been working on our own practice of saying "no," and we realize how challenging it can be. Reflecting on our own experiments with flexing our Ditty-Ditching muscles, we know that there's always a relational context for every "no." And as much as we strive to simplify our "nos," disentangling them from apologies, justifications, and Magic Wand waving, we're always navigating the realities of the relationship and situation of where the ask is coming from. While "no" is indeed a complete sentence, it's also helpful to have a range of responses to help you build the right sized "no" for your situation. We think of it as scaling our "no" to fit the circumstance.

When thinking about scaling our "no," we need to consider two important variables:

1. The amount of crazy in the Ditty that someone is trying to hand us.

2. The number of Ditties this person has handed us in the past.

Let's consider the first variable: the Ditty itself. Is the Ditty something simple, such as donating a dozen cupcakes for a school fundraiser? Or is it something more outrageous, like organizing and running a dozen bake sales every evening for the next two months? The actual content of the ask is important to take into consideration when delivering our "no."

Next, we consider the person who's trying to hand us the Ditty by asking ourselves what kind of Ditty Distributor they are. We define these folks as:

Ditty Distributor

/didē/ / /dəˈstribyədər/ *proper noun*
1. a person who passes along their Ditties to others
2. one who continually leaves unwanted and unnecessary tasks for others in their wake

Are they an infrequent Ditty Distributor or a high-volume Ditty Distributor? (In Part 6, we'll invite you to reflect on how to prevent yourself from becoming a Ditty Distributor to others.) You know the difference between these two types of people in your life. There are those who seldom, if ever, ask us to pick up a Ditty. Perhaps this request is the first time they're turning to us with a Ditty in hand. These are individuals whom we prioritize preserving a relationship with over the long term.

Compare this person to others in your life who seem to constantly be leaving a wave of Ditties in their wake. They produce Ditties like confetti in Times Square on New Year's Eve. We see them coming down the hall in the office and we flip off the light and dive under our desks to avoid them; their name pops up on our caller ID and we immediately hit "ignore" so as not to get drowned by the Ditty monsoon we know awaits us on the other end of the line; we spot them in the aisle at the grocery store and we try to pretend we're in the witness relocation program, pulling a box of cereal off the shelf to cover our face.

Looking at the intersection of these two variables, we've created a scaled level of "no" responses—where the tone of delivery is just as important as the words themselves. Tone encompasses the emotion and intent behind your words, shaping how your message is received. For example, a warm and empathetic tone can soften the blow of a refusal, showing that you care about the other person's feelings even as you stand firm in your decision. On the other hand, a hesitant or overly apologetic tone can undermine your message, making your "no" seem uncertain and less likely to be respected. A neutral or detached tone can communicate that your decision is final and not up for debate. Mastering the appropriate tone is crucial; it ensures your "no" is not only clear but also received in the spirit it's intended. Understanding the nuances of tone can help you navigate difficult conversations more effectively. Whether you're dealing with a close friend, a colleague, or a casual acquaintance, using the right tone can make all the difference in how your "no" is perceived and respected.

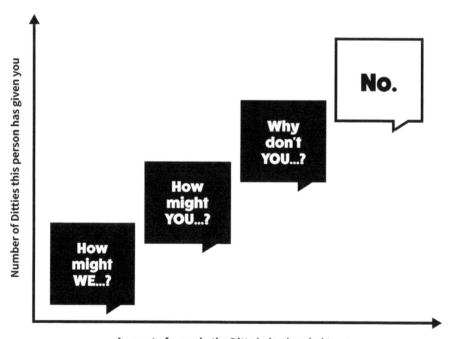

Amount of crazy in the Ditty being handed to you

Let's unpack each of these levels of "no," shall we?

Level 1: "No, but how might WE...?"

Tone = Comforting, like you'd use with a teary child who just inadvertently dropped their ice cream cone for the first time and you're willing to help them get a new one.

This is for those times when you still want to be involved in being helpful following your "no." While you're not willing to take on the entire Ditty they offer, you are willing to handle a specific part of it and collaborate with them to find a solution for the rest.

For instance, instead of agreeing to take on the entire project at work, you might say "no" to managing the project but "yes" to handling a specific task within it, such as creating a presentation or analyzing data. By doing this, you maintain your boundaries while still contributing positively. It's about finding a middle ground. This approach allows you to stay involved and supportive without overextending yourself.

Being helpful here is different from the Ditching Dynamic of The Magic Wand. The key lies in balance and intention. Here, you deliver a clear "no," set boundaries, offer help within your capacity, respect your limits, and empower others to take responsibility for their own problems. In contrast, The Magic Wand takes on too much, feeling compelled to fix others' issues beyond what's needed or asked—offering to do x, y, z, and every other letter in the alphabet—leading to burnout and resentment. Instead, by offering targeted assistance like "I can't do x, but I can help with y," you encourage independence and avoid overextending yourself, keeping a healthy balance between helping others and caring for your own needs.

Level 2: "No, but how might YOU...?"

Tone = Firm, like you'd use with a child who dropped their ice cream cone for the second time, and you're coaching them on how to avoid doing it again in the future.

This is for those times when you want to be helpful but not directly involved following your "no." You aren't willing to take on any piece of the Ditty, but you still care enough to suggest actions they might take to resolve their need. In this scenario, you're offering guidance from a distance—perhaps recommending resources, suggesting alternative solutions, or pointing them toward someone who might be able to help. It's about providing support without compromising your own boundaries, ensuring they feel acknowledged and assisted without dragging yourself into their problem.

For instance, instead of agreeing to take on an additional project at work—or helping them tackle a piece of it—you might offer to help them brainstorm ideas or connect them with someone who has the expertise they need. You're being helpful without directly being involved.

Level 3: "No. Why don't YOU...?"

> *Tone = Stern, like you'd use with a child who purposely dropped their ice cream cone for the third time, and you tell them that if they want another ice cream, they need to save their money and buy it themselves.*

This is for those times when you've already said "no" multiple times or you've offered prior help that was ignored. You're done playing the helpful ally and you've even set down your Magic Wand as you have no interest in holding the Ditty they're offering. Frankly, you don't really care if they figure out their issue or not. In these situations, you've recognized your limits and are deciding not to invest any more energy into a situation where your efforts aren't appreciated or necessary. You're prioritizing your well-being, making sure your time and resources go toward things that truly matter to you. Sometimes, it's perfectly fine to let others fend for themselves while you kick back and enjoy your peace of mind.

Level 4: "No."

> *Tone = Confidently unarguable and clear in its delivery, like you'd use with a child who dropped their ice cream for the 10th time. Not only are you not replacing it, you don't want them to even ask, "Why?"*

Sometimes we need to simply remember that "no" is indeed a complete sentence, and that's all you need. Imagine if your friend asks you to help them move right after you've just broken your leg. You give them a pointed look at your cast and simply say, "No." Or picture your coworker asking you to take on their project right after you've just been assigned a huge, urgent task by your boss due at the end of the day. You give them a knowing look and simply say, "No." No explanations needed—no justifications, just a simple, firm "no." Mastering this straightforward response is like a superpower, setting clear boundaries and communicating your decision without leaving any room for debate. By using this clear and resolute "no" in these situations, you skip the unnecessary back-and-forth, respect your own boundaries, and get your point across with authority and clarity.

BONUS: The Spinal Tap[143] Level 11 "Hell No!"

Tone = Absolutely unambiguous and final, shutting down the ask and deterring the asker from ever bringing up such a request again. This is for the kid you never want to ask you for another ice cream cone again—ever.

This "no" is the mic drop of declines, the atomic bomb of rejections—it's a definitive, unapologetic refusal of not only this task but any others like it in the future. When you deliver this kind of atomic "no," it's like slamming the door shut on a pesky salesperson—you're not interested, and you want them to know it loud and clear.

This "no" doesn't leave any room for misunderstanding; it's a statement of absolute finality. However, be aware that this level of refusal can burn bridges and leave smoldering ashes in its wake, so make sure you're ready to drop that bomb. But if you're looking to shut down a request with authority and certainty while also deterring the Ditty Distributor from ever darkening your door again, this kind of atomic "no" is your weapon of choice.

We invite you to come up with your own symbolic name for this "no" in your life. We call it a "Mc-God-No!" (an amalgamation of our last names), which creates a very vibrant moniker for when we want to signal to ourselves that something is a 100%, resolute, no-ifs-ands-or-buts "No!"

The Ultimate No-saurus: A Dictionary of Declines

The art of scaling our "no" is something we're constantly practicing. We've found that having a variety of "no" responses ready helps us confidently face any request. Inspired by our conversations with women and our own experiences, we've created *The Ultimate No-saurus: A thesaurus of "no" responses.* This collection offers 10 different ways to say "no," each tailored to help you gracefully navigate those tricky situations where declining a Ditty is necessary. The examples align with the five levels of "no" outlined above, ranging from collaborative refusals to firm rejections. With this handy guide, you'll never again be at a loss for words when it's time to Ditch Ditties, regardless of the distributor!

NO LEVEL	THE GOAL	EXAMPLES	
1. No, but how might WE...?	You're declining but still offering to brainstorm or help them find a solution.	**The Team Player No**	• No, I can't take on the entire project, but how might we divide the tasks and tackle it as a team? • No, I can't finish this report for you, but how might we get you started? I can help you outline the main points to get you going.
		The Good Friend No	• No, I can't help you move this weekend, but you might consider asking Sam—they might be willing to help! • No, I can't lend you my car this weekend, but my partner's car is available, and I can ask if they can lend it to you.

THE DYNAMICS OF DITCHING & SCALING YOUR "NO"

NO LEVEL	THE GOAL	EXAMPLES	
2: No, but how might YOU...?	You're saying "no" but encouraging them to find their own solution.	**The Did-You-Try...? No**	• No, I can't babysit tonight; how might you tap into your local network to see who can help? • No, I don't have that info right now; did you give Google a whirl?
		The You-Got-This No	• No, I can't write your essay for you, but you might want to start with an outline. It'll make the writing process much easier for you. • No, I can't cover your shift, but who else could you ask? I'm sure someone wants to pick up some overtime.
3: No. Why don't YOU...?"	A firmer "no" while offering suggestions for them to pursue on their own.	**The DIY No**	• No, I can't stay late to help with the presentation, but why don't you try using the new presentation software we discussed? It's quite user-friendly. • No, I can't cook dinner tonight, but why don't you try that new recipe you found? I'm sure you'll do a great job.

NO LEVEL	THE GOAL	EXAMPLES	
3: No. Why don't YOU...?	A firmer "no" while offering suggestions for them to pursue on their own.	**The Pass-the-Baton No**	• No, I can't help you paint the house this weekend, but why don't you see if Aunt Lisa can lend a hand? • No, I can't assist with the report right now, but why don't you ask Anne? She just finished a similar project.
4: No	A clear and straightfor-ward refusal without fur-ther explana-tion.	**The Polite Pass**	• I'm flattered you thought of me, but no, I have to pass. I wish you the best of luck with it! • Thanks for asking, but no.
		The Straight Shooter No	• No. I can't stay late today. • No. You can't use my car. • No. I can't babysit for you. • No. I'm not available for that. • No.

NO LEVEL	THE GOAL	EXAMPLES	
11: Hell No!	A definitive refusal that annihilates the current and future requests completely.	**The Nuclear No**	• No. I won't sacrifice my weekends for work anymore. If you ask again, I will report you to HR. • Absolutely not—I'm not lending you that much money and don't ever ask me again.
		The Drop-the-Mic No	• No. I'm not your go-to for last-minute favors. Quit treating me like your assistant. • No. I'm not your personal chauffeur. Stop asking me. • No. I'm not handling your responsibilities. This is the last time I'll say it.

We're sure you have your own entries to add to *The Ultimate No-saurus*! Take the time to practice and develop your own unique ways to say "no." Each situation and relationship may call for a different approach, and the more you practice, the more natural it will feel to let that little word roll off your tongue.

As you fine-tune your "no" game, remember that its power lies in delivery and clarity. Each level of "no" is designed to help you balance setting boundaries while keeping relationships intact. Whether you go for a team player approach or drop an emphatic refusal, the goal is to empower yourself to say "no" with unapologetic confidence to any Ditty that crosses your path.

Part 5 Ditty-Ditching Duhs

Here are some key takeaways for mastering the art of scaling your "no":

1. **You Can Serve Up a "No" Without a Side of Sorry, Worry, or a Magic Wand:** It's common to feel like you need to pad your "no" with apologies, worries, or offers of extra magical help. However, your "no" doesn't need any embellishments. Remember, "no" can stand alone as a complete sentence if you let it.

2. **Not Every "No" Needs to Sound the Same:** While "No" is a complete sentence, each "no" can be tailored to the situation and individual. Some situations require a firm "no," while others benefit from a gentler approach. Understanding this helps us deliver "nos" with the appropriate tone and context. Refer to the "no" scale to choose the right type of refusal—from collaborative to emphatic, depending on the context.

3. **Just Like an Acquired Taste, Learning to Say "No" Gets Better the More You Try It:** Just like Dr. Seuss's character Sam-I-Am initially resisted green eggs and ham, you might resist saying "no" and Ditching Ditties at first. It's an acquired taste, but once you try it, you'll enjoy saying "no" and Ditching in the dark, in the park, in the rain, or on a train. You'll love Ditching here and there—you'll love Ditching anywhere![144]

PART 6
The Advanced Ditty-Ditching Academy

CONGRATULATIONS!

With your added skill of learning how to scale your "no," you're ready to Ditch Ditties like a pro! But, as with anything meaningful in life, there's always more to learn. We trust that you're not surprised by this news. In this section, we want to showcase some of the advanced Ditty-Ditching techniques we've been experimenting with. We invite you to practice these—as well as develop your own unique Ditching moves—so that you can find yourself embracing a state of mind where no Ditty stands a chance of dragging you down!

Our top five advanced Ditty-Ditching skills include:

1. **The Ditty Detox:** Ditching Current Ditties

2. **The Ditty Defense Drill:** Avoiding Ditty Distributors

3. **The Ditty Delegation Dance:** Turning Your Ditty into Another's Delight

4. **The Ditty Metamorphosis:** Evolving Ditties & Deeds into Delights and Preventing Duties from Becoming Ditties

5. **The Ditching Assist:** Supporting Other Ditty-Ditching Divas

The Ditty Detox: Ditching Current Ditties

In earlier sections you learned how to recognize Ditties—including ones that present themselves with Ditty Disguises—and how to begin saying "no" to new Ditties that come your way. We're guessing it's also safe to assume you have a few (or few hundred) current Ditties you'd like to Ditch.

Getting rid of a current Ditty on your plate can be a little different from not picking up a new one in the first place. Saying "no" to something you've already said "yes" to can be particularly challenging due to our fear of disappointing others and the sense of obligation that comes when we've made a commitment. Once you've agreed to do something, there's an expectation from both you and others that you'll follow through. Backtracking on that agreement can lead to feelings of guilt, anxiety, and fear of judgment. And let's not forget that The Persistent Pleaser dynamic is going to raise her head and sing loudly in our ear: *You don't want them to be upset, do you?* Additionally, there may be practical considerations such as time and effort already invested in the commitment, making it harder to let go. Overcoming these challenges requires courage, clear communication, and a willingness to prioritize your own well-being, even if it means feeling like we're disappointing others in the process.

When it comes to flipping that original "yes" into a "no," we invite you to first give yourself a pat on the back for having the guts to reassess the situation and own your awareness that this is in fact a Ditty you want to Ditch. You're on your way to earning your Ditching doctorate simply by recognizing those things that you no longer want to give energy to.

Now, when it's time to drop the news to others that you're evolving your original acceptance into a Ditch, there's not a one-size-fits-all way to do this (are you surprised?!). Just like we explored in Part 5 with scaling your "no," you'll be balancing the impact of this Ditch on the relationship as well as yourself. Depending on the situation, you may feel a need to be apologetic or helpful in finding an alternative solution for them. At the same time, we invite you to be aware of The Apologetic Angel and The Magic Wand dynamics we explored earlier. There are indeed times and places for an authentic "I'm sorry" and an offer to help in alternative ways—just make sure these responses are authentic and not another Ditty in and of themselves.

For many women, distinguishing between authentic apologies or the desire to be helpful and our conditioned habitual reactions can be challenging. Authentic apologies come from a place of genuine regret or empathy, reflecting a true understanding of the situation and its impact on the other person. These apologies are often accompanied by sincere offers to make amends or find constructive solutions. For example, if you missed an important meeting that affected your team's progress, you might genuinely feel bad and offer to handle additional tasks or reschedule to make things right. On the other hand, habitual reactions occur when you automatically say "sorry" without much thought or genuine feeling behind it, such as lightly bumping into someone in the hallway. To discern between the two, consider if you truly feel remorseful or empathetic about the situation and if your apology is necessary and meaningful. Authentic apologies deal with the actual situation and its effects, while habitual "I'm sorrys" and "Here, let me help..." are often just automatic responses. Understanding this difference can help us make sure our responses are genuine and not just a way to please others.

Apology needed or not, we each have our own stories of Ditching current Ditties in our lives. For example:

The Ditty Diaries: Miriam's Story

A while back, a colleague invited me to join an online class they were teaching as an observer. Initially, I was enthusiastic about the opportunity to learn something new. However, the reality of late-night sessions and repetitive content quickly turned it into more of a chore than a Delight. After skipping a couple of classes, I realized this commitment wasn't aligning with my needs or interests.

Instead of ghosting my colleague, I decided to communicate openly with her. To my surprise, she was relieved to hear my honest feedback and was supportive of me reclaiming my time for other things. I didn't even need to apologize—which was new for me! This experience taught me the value of being honest about my commitments and needs, rather than just going along to please others.

If only every Ditch of an existing Ditty were as easy, right?

To help expand your Dictionary of Declines from Part 5, we offer the following possible "No-After-a-Yes" responses you can play with in different situations. We also invite you to create your own entries in this never-ending dictionary!

- **The Reconsidered Refusal:** Politely express that upon further reflection, you've realized that you're unable to commit to the task or obligation. For example, *"After thinking it over, I realize I won't be able to do justice to this project right now."*

- **The Changed Circumstance Decline:** Explain that unforeseen circumstances have arisen that prevent you from fulfilling your initial agreement. For instance, *"Unfortunately, my schedule has unexpectedly become much busier, and I won't be able to follow through as planned."*

- **The Priority Pivot:** Emphasize that new priorities require your immediate attention, making it impossible to fulfill your previous commitment. You could say, *"Due to some urgent matters that have come up, I need to prioritize other tasks at the moment."*

- **The Call-in-Well Ditch:** Simply be honest and admit that you made a mistake in agreeing in the first place. One of our mentors advised us to "call in well" when we realize we've accepted a responsibility that, upon further reflection, wasn't the wisest choice. She would say, "Lots of people call in sick, but you need to call in well. Tell them you were sick when you said 'yes,' and now that you're feeling better, you realize you should have said 'no.'"

A Bite-Size Challenge

Create your own entry for a "No-After-a-Yes" response and imagine different ways to gracefully back out of commitments you now realize are Ditties. What's one situation where you feel a "No-After-a-Yes" response could be particularly useful for you?

The Ditty Defense Drill: Avoiding Ditty Distributors & Preventing Yourself From Becoming One

Ditching unwanted Ditties is a critical skill, but learning to avoid them in the first place is just as important. Managing or avoiding Ditty Distributors in our lives is key, as we broke down in Part 5. It's easy to joke about Ditty Distributors, but recognizing who they are is crucial. These individuals subtly pile on tasks and expectations we may not want or have the capacity to handle, often making their requests seem urgent or essential. As women, we may be especially susceptible to Ditty Distributors due to our tendencies toward The Persistent Pleaser or The Perfect Pearl dynamics. Noticing both the Ditties *and* their sources helps us protect our time and energy more effectively.

Here are our top five signals that someone is a Ditty Distributor:

1. **The Frequent Favor Asker:** They consistently ask for your help, time, or resources without considering your availability. They're always popping up with requests of all shapes and sizes. You know what they sound like: *"I hate to ask for one more thing from you, but you're so good at everything, could you just take a quick look? Oh, yeah, and after you do that, can you help me with this...and then this...?"*

2. **The One-Way Requester:** These folks rarely, if ever, offer help or support in return for the favors they ask of you, leav-

ing you feeling like you're perpetually expected to play Santa in the holiday of their life. Perhaps you've heard echoes like *"I need your help with this; I'm just so swamped with other tasks."*

3. **The Just-a-Little Justifier:** These folks are masters at downplaying requests, making them sound like the tiniest of favors. They minimize the ask, framing it as something inconsequential, hoping you'll acquiesce without much thought. Their persuasion tactics involve phrases like *"It's just a quick favor"* or *"It'll only take a minute of your time."*

4. **The Bewitcher:** These are individuals who possess a magical charm that makes their requests feel like delightful invitations rather than burdensome asks. Somehow, they weave a spell that makes it seem like fulfilling their wishes is simply the natural course of action. Their subtle approach might include phrases like *"Wouldn't it be wonderful if...?"* or *"I thought you might enjoy joining me in..."* They somehow sprinkle pixie dust with their words, blinding us to the Ditty behind the glitter.

5. **The Heartstring Tugger:** These are individuals who may guilt-trip or pressure you into saying "yes" to their demands by playing the emotional card to get their way. They use different versions of *"If you cared about me, you'd help me with this. I thought I could count on you"* (sometimes with the added gut punch of *"I guess I was wrong."*).

As with so many things we've explored so far, awareness of these people and their tendencies to deliver Ditties in our lives is an important step toward interrupting our habit of saying "yes" to things we don't really want or need to do. When we become more aware of these signals, we can respond appropriately. Perhaps returning to scaling your "no" and pulling out your own Level 11 "Atomic No" as appropriate.

Becoming aware of these tendencies also provides a mirror for you to look at yourself! That's right, any of us—even YOU—can be a Ditty Distributor. In fact, one of the three of us writing this book is an *expert* Bewitcher (we'll let you guess who that is). Take a moment to tune in to how often you're asking for favors or piling tasks on others—at work, at home, with friends, etc. Would others describe you as a "task tornado," leaving a trail of to-dos in your wake? Do you ask the same people for things over and over? Do you respect others' "nos," or do you pull at those heartstrings and inadvertently put pressure on others to comply with your asks? By becoming more aware of your own behavior and how it's landing on others, you can dodge the Ditty Distributor label (if you want to).

When dealing with people who are Ditty Distributors—especially if they're high-volume ones—don't be afraid to playfully call them out. A light-hearted comment like "Are you trying to set a record for how many tasks you can hand out?" can get the point across without causing tension. At home, if a family member is always piling chores on you, you might say, "Is this a chore relay race? Because I'm out of breath!" You can also make it a game—suggest a "no challenge," where everyone tries to say "no" at least once a day. Encouraging open conversations about workload and expectations can help everyone feel more comfortable with setting limits and respecting each other's capacity. This way, you turn a potentially awkward situation into a supportive way to manage everyone's time and energy better.

A Bite-Size Challenge

Identify the people who frequently distribute Ditties to you. These could be colleagues passing off extra work, friends making persistent requests, or family members expecting favors. Imagine you have a "Ditty Deflector Shield" the next time they come to you with a request. What will be your go-to response to let them know you're on a Ditty diet right now and must pass?

The Ditty Delegation Dance: Turning Your Ditty Into Another's Delight

We want to let you in on another little-known secret in the world of Ditching. By declining what doesn't spark joy for us, we're not just saving our own sanity, we're creating space for others who may genuinely enjoy or excel at those activities. That's right…

One person's Ditty is another's Delight!

Just because you'd rather poke your eye out with a hot poker than do certain tasks and asks doesn't mean that others wouldn't *love* to do those exact things! Consider this: Offering tasks we dislike to those who may handle them better isn't just savvy, it's kind. It enables us to concentrate on our strengths while granting others the opportunity to showcase their expertise. Whether in our personal or professional realms, reallocating responsibilities based on individual strengths and interests not only enhances our own joy but also encourages others to do the same.

This isn't just a lofty dream for Ditching unwanted tasks; it's a practical approach to streamlining your life, both personally and professionally. Take, for instance, this example from our colleagues who transformed the concept of undesirable tasks into an office strategy.

The Ditty Diaries: Zara's Story

I remember a time in our office when we were drowning in undesirable tasks that nobody wanted to handle. You know the type: tedious, low-energy duties that sap your motivation. It was becoming a real problem, and the morale in our team was starting to dip. So, a few of us decided to transform these tasks into an office strategy.

We started by periodically gathering all these dreaded tasks and crafting a job description for a new position around them. Instead of just reassigning these tasks to already overwhelmed team members, we took a different approach. We actively sought out individuals who actually enjoyed doing these types of tasks.

To our surprise, there was always someone eager to tackle what others considered burdensome. I remember when we first tried this, we found Sarah, a meticulous organizer who found joy in detailed data entry and scheduling—tasks that most of us found mind-numbingly boring. She was thrilled to take on these responsibilities, and it created a win-win scenario for everyone involved.

This strategy not only improved overall productivity but also boosted morale. Sarah was happy doing what she loved, and the rest of us could focus on tasks that energized us. It was a perfect example of turning a potentially negative situation into a positive one, simply by rethinking how we approached the problem.

We also heard this approach bubble up in some people's personal lives, like in this story:

The Ditty Diaries: Nikki's Story

I remember a time when I found myself constantly fielding my teenage son's requests, from homework help to weekend activities. It felt like every minute of my day was consumed by his needs, and it was starting to wear me down. I also noticed that this constant interaction was causing a disconnect between my husband and our son. My husband seemed to be on the sidelines, and I was the default parent for everything.

Realizing this, I made a conscious decision to step back and allow my husband to take the lead in responding to our son's requests and spending more time with him. It wasn't easy at first. Every time my son asked for help or wanted to do something, my instinct was to jump in and take charge. But I knew I had to resist the urge to intervene at every opportunity.

Gradually, as I learned to say "no" (even if unspoken), something amazing happened. My husband and son started to develop a stronger connection. My husband stepped up and found new ways to bond with our son, whether it was helping with homework or planning weekend activities. It was heartwarming to see their relationship grow.

Meanwhile, I found myself with more time to focus on other things. I could finally catch up on my hobbies, spend time with friends, and even just relax without feeling guilty. My decision to create space for my husband to say "yes" in new ways not only strengthened their bond but also brought a much-needed balance to our family dynamics.

We've experienced firsthand how our own unwanted Ditties can turn into Delights for others. Remember Molly's story where she reluctantly took on the role of president for a local volunteer board and eventually realized it was a Ditty wrapped in the disguise of a Veiled Threat? Well, here's the rest of that story!

The Ditty Diary: Molly's Story...Continued

For years, I felt de-energized by the never-ending responsibilities of this volunteer role, and it became a burdensome Ditty in my life. The constant demands and lack of appreciation started to weigh heavily on me.

I was always afraid if I stepped down the organization would be left in disarray. But eventually as I began sharing that I was contemplating stepping down, I discovered someone else was eager to lead. It was a revelation. By passing the torch, I not only freed myself from the overwhelming duties but also opened the door for someone else to thrive in a role they were genuinely excited about.

Letting go of this burdensome Ditty allowed me to reclaim my time and energy, and it gave someone else the opportunity to shine. It was a win-win situation, and I learned the importance of recognizing when it's time to step back and let others step up.

These stories illustrate the power of clarity in shedding unwanted Ditties and making room for others to find their Delights. Remember, what feels like a chore to you might be a thrill for someone else. By swapping, sharing, and reimagining tasks when appropriate, we can focus on our Essentials, making life more enjoyable and less Ditty-filled for everyone.

A Bite-Size Challenge

As you work to delegate things that feel like Ditties to you but Delights to others, ask yourself:

→ What tasks am I currently tackling (whether at home, work, or in my community) that drain my energy but that someone else might actually find delightful?

→ How can I tap into my network to discover someone who'd genuinely enjoy taking on a task I've received but am not keen on doing?

→ How might I involve people I live with in tasks I've typically handled solo, allowing them to bring their own flair and joy to the mix?

→ Could I propose a task exchange with someone else who has different preferences—a fun "Ditty for a Delight" swap that benefits us both?

The Ditty Metamorphosis: Evolving Things Into Delights & Preventing Things From Becoming Ditties

In the advanced realm of Ditty Ditching, it's important to recognize that sometimes the tasks we initially perceive as Ditties—and even some of our Duties—can be reframed into opportunities for things we actually *do* want. By shifting our perspective, we can turn seemingly mundane or burdensome tasks into meaningful experiences or avenues for personal growth. This shift in mindset lets us turn potential drudgery into purposeful action, making our lives more enjoyable and helping us grow personally.

For this lesson, we drew inspiration from one of our mothers' experiences with a family wedding.

The Ditty Diaries: Hattie's Story

At the prospect of attending my grand-nephew's wedding, I initially felt a wave of reluctance wash over me. The thought of the long drive and the obligatory social interactions dampened my spirits as I contemplated whether to RSVP "yes" or "no." However, as I pondered the situation further, a subtle shift occurred in my perspective. Rather than viewing the event solely as a burdensome obligation of cake eating and silly small talk with people who could care less if I was there or not, I began to see it as an opportunity to connect with my aging sister, who I knew would be attending. With this realization, the wedding transformed from a mere obligation on the calendar into a chance to create cherished memories with my sister. My decision to attend was no longer driven by a sense of duty but by the prospect of meaningful moments spent with her, making the journey not only bearable but also filled with the potential for delight.

As this story illustrates, sometimes, evolving something from a Ditty or Duty into a Delight can be a matter of perspective (we introduced this with the Bite-Size Challenge on page 34, asking you to do Duties "your way"). While Ditty metamorphosis is indeed an advanced practice to play with, it is important to recognize that not everything can—nor should— be reframed, hence the importance of flexing those Ditching muscles.

On one hand, there are moments that can be reframed in a meaningful way, like seeing an obligatory family event as a chance to connect with loved ones. On the other hand, while reframing can transform some obligations into opportunities, there are burdens or by-products of our gendered, patriarchal culture—like a female leader being asked to hold a man's bag at a conference—that shouldn't be sugarcoated. These moments are not just minor inconveniences; they're often subtle reinforcements of outdated gender norms and expectations that perpetuate inequality.

Understanding the difference is crucial. When we reframe too much, we risk falling into familiar traps of accepting too much simply because we want to be, or are expected to be, positive as women. It's important to recognize when an obligation is an unfair burden rather than an opportunity for growth or connection. For us, three clues that something should **not** be reframed include:

1. **Double Standards:** If the task or obligation reinforces unfair gender roles, stereotypes, or inequality, it's a sign that reframing might not be appropriate. For example, being asked to perform menial tasks (including taking the notes in a meeting) simply because of your gender is a situation where saying "no" is more empowering than trying to find a positive spin.

2. **Un-Well-being:** When a task or obligation significantly impacts your mental, emotional, or physical well-being, it's important to recognize the need to prioritize self-care over reframing. If the activity leaves you feeling drained, stressed, or resentful, it's a strong indicator that it's time to flex those Ditching muscles instead of trying to reframe the situation.

3. **Moochers Mooching:** If the request comes from someone who consistently takes advantage of your willingness to help without showing appreciation or reciprocation, it's a sign that you should not reframe the situation. Relationships should be built on mutual respect and give-and-take. If you're always the one giving and rarely receiving, it's better to set boundaries rather than trying to see the bright side.

As we advance our Ditching skills, we learn when to say "no" and understand that while reframing is helpful when possible, it shouldn't come at the expense of our well-being or reinforce negative patterns.

A Bite-Size Challenge

Think about the Ditties and Duties you are currently juggling. Explore potential Duty-to-Delight transformations by asking yourself:

→ What aspect of this can I genuinely enjoy or find meaning in?

→ How can I incorporate my personal strengths or interests into this task?

→ Can I reframe this as an opportunity for personal growth or skill development?

→ How might completing this task contribute to my long-term goals or values?

→ Is there a way to make this task more enjoyable or rewarding for myself?

On the flip side, however, we also must be mindful that evolution can go both ways. Deeds, Duties—and even Delights—can shift into Ditties if we're not mindful!

Preventing an agreement from morphing into an unwanted Ditty requires clarity up front. Without a clear understanding of what we're agreeing to, even the simplest tasks can snowball into burdensome obligations. Taking the time to clarify key components of an agreement is crucial, even though it may initially feel uncomfortable, especially for those who are inclined to be The Persistent Pleaser. However, investing the effort to ensure mutual understanding up front can save considerable time and frustration later. By openly discussing expectations, responsibilities, and potential outcomes, we can align with others on our understanding of the agreement and avoid misunderstandings or unanticipated Ditties down the road. Inspired by Brené Brown's declaration that "clear is kind,"[145] we've found checking to see if an agreement is C-L-E-A-R helps keep things from devolving into Ditties. For us, this means it is:

- **C= Comprehensive.** Ask yourself: Does the agreement cover all relevant aspects of the task and roles with no details left in ambiguity?

- **L= Logical.** Ask yourself: Does the agreement make sense and follow a rational flow, with everyone understanding their roles and responsibilities?

- **E= Empowering.** Ask yourself: Does the agreement empower everyone involved to fulfill their responsibilities as needed?

- **A= Adaptable.** Ask yourself: Does the agreement allow for adjustments if circumstances change?

- **R= Realistic.** Ask yourself: Does the agreement seem feasible with realistic expectations and timelines?

No matter what you're doing or whom you're doing it for, keep tabs on yourself over time to make sure that the task is still manageable and aligns with your priorities. If it starts feeling overwhelming or draining, don't hesitate to speak up and renegotiate your commitment or to ask for help. By staying transparent and looking out for your well-being, you can keep things from turning into an unwanted Ditty.

The Ditching Assist: Supporting Other Ditching Divas

Ditching Ditties does not have to be a solo sport. In fact, we've found that we're better Ditchers when we lean on each other. As women, we hold the power to be authentic mirrors and pillars of support for one another as we navigate the complexities of our lives. Who else will best understand and help us unravel the dynamics we each navigate in our own ways, including our Persistent Pleaser, Perfect Pearl, Self-Doubting Dame, Apologizing Angel, Magic Wand, and Ruminating Ruby tendencies?

Some of the best Ditching assist moves we've discovered in our own Ditching journeys include:

- **"Do-You-Really?" Mirrors:** Imagine this: You're chatting with your friend over a cup of coffee, and she's contemplating taking on yet another task that she's not particularly excited about. As her faithful mirror, you raise an eyebrow and ask, *"Do you really want to do that?"* with a knowing grin. She pauses, pondering your question. Suddenly, the light bulb flickers on, and she realizes she was ready to say "yes" once again out of habit, not because it aligns with her true desires. With your gentle nudge, she starts to see through the fog of obligation, reclaiming her power to choose. Next week, the roles may be reversed, where she's the one asking you a lovingly irreverent *"Do you really?"* when you're pondering an unwanted task on your plate.

- **Story Swappers:** Unlike *Fight Club*,[146] the first rule of Ditching Ditties is to talk about Ditching Ditties. By sharing our stories and insights with each other, we can inspire and uplift one another in both our personal and professional spheres. At minimum, sharing our stories helps us to look at, and even laugh at, the sometimes-ridiculous dynamics and situations we face as women. Sharing our stories can also help us see our Ditties in a new light, challenging us to reframe difficult situations as opportunities and empowering us to discover creative solutions, including new ways to say "no" and "yes" with confidence. If anything, it helps us realize that we are **NOT** in fact alone on this journey of womanhood.

- **Celebrators & Elevators:** No pom-poms needed (unless you want them), as there are many ways we can support each other as Ditty Ditchers. This move is all about recognizing and applauding each other's successes and milestones along the way. It involves offering genuine praise, encouragement, and validation for others' efforts in saying "no," pausing perfection, and reclaiming their time and energy. As celebrators and elevators, we lift each other up, boost each other's confidence, and shine a spotlight on our achievements, no matter how big or small the Ditch may be.

A Bite-Size Challenge

Who are the Ditty-Ditching Divas on your speed dial? Think of all the women in your life you go to—or could go to—for support when making a decision about an opportunity. Create a note in your phone with their:

→ Name

→ Contact Details

→ Relationship to You

→ Strengths They Bring to Support You

Do they know they're part of your Ditching crew? Let them know the role they play and what this means! Consider the support you can bring to their Ditching Journey. Leverage this list often, because we can't go it alone! Your Ditty-Ditching Divas will always be on tap to help you make those important decisions to Ditch a Ditty or take on a Delight.

By honing these five advanced Ditty-Ditching moves, including the Ditty Detox, Ditty Defense Drill, Ditty Delegation Dance, Ditty Metamorphosis, and Ditching Assist, you're on your way to earning your black belt in Ditching! With each practice, you'll become more adept at shedding unwanted tasks, deflecting requests from Ditty Distributors, turning Duties into Delights, reframing challenges, and supporting fellow Ditchers.

As you practice these techniques, think of it like becoming a master gardener: you're weeding out the unwanted tasks and obligations that clutter your life, allowing what matters most to blossom.

Part 6 Ditty-Ditching Duhs

Life is full of endless opportunities to practice our advanced Ditty-Ditching moves. With every new challenge and request, we can refine our skills—and build new ones—ensuring that we stay focused on what truly matters. Here are some insights we hope you take with you along the way.

1. **Does Practice Make Perfect?:** We don't believe in perfection, at least not the version The Perfect Pearl aspires to. Yet, through regular practice and the deliberate application of Ditching strategies, we can build our Ditty-Ditching muscles and shape the life we genuinely want.

2. **DIY Ditching Drills:** Try and create the Ditty-Ditching fitness routine that's best for you! Here are a few things we've covered that you can use in your rotation:
   - **The Ditty Detox:** Keep practicing techniques to identify and eliminate current Ditties in your life.
   - **The Ditty Defense Drill:** Continue honing strategies to avoid Ditty Distributors and protect your time.
   - **The Ditty Delegation Dance:** Explore ways to turn your unwanted tasks into someone else's Delight.
   - **The Ditty Metamorphosis:** Work on transforming burdensome asks or tasks into enjoyable undertakings, preventing new Ditties from forming.
   - **The Ditching Assist:** Support fellow Ditching Divas in their journey and ask for their support as well.

3. **You're Your Best Teacher:** Pay attention to what strategies work for you and which don't. Embrace your unique approach and don't be afraid to create your own signature Ditching moves.

PART 7
The Ditty-Ditching Diva Dynamics & Living Happily Ever Along

Welcome to the sisterhood of Ditty-Ditching Divas—no secret handshake required! You've earned your place here by learning to recognize your Essentials and prioritize what matters most to you.

We've arrived at the final section of the book, and what an incredible journey it has been! Throughout these pages, we've delved into the unique dynamics we face as women, explored the art of scaling our "no," shared heartfelt stories, and honed our skills in Ditching those unwanted Ditties that drain your energy. As we celebrate your new title as a Ditty-Ditching Diva, let's take a moment to explain what that truly means by looking at our very last set of dynamics. After diving deep into women's stories who seem to embody these traits, we've identified what we refer to as the **Diva Dynamics**.

We define a Diva Dynamic as:

Diva Dynamic

/ˈdēvə/ dīˈnamik/ *noun*

1. an internalized clarity that helps us evaluate requests clearly and confidently
2. an awareness that ensures we respond to asks in ways that align with what matters most

The top three Diva Dynamics we've discovered include:

1. **The Clear Crystal**

2. **The Self-Confident Sage**

3. **The Wondering Woman**

Diva Dynamic: The Clear Crystal

Oprah Winfrey, a diva by any measure, once said:

"When you don't know what to do, my best advice is to do nothing until clarity comes. Getting still, being able to hear your own voice and not the voices of the world, quickens clarity. Once you decide what you want, you make a commitment to that decision."[147]

We've learned that:

- Studies show that when women have a clear understanding of what they value, they're more likely to feel that their actions are meaningful and impactful, which further strengthens their confidence.[148]

- A lack of clarity has been identified as one saboteur of self-confidence.[149]

- Clarity has been shown to help interrupt destructive perfectionism.[150]

- Research has shown that women leaders are more self-aware than their male counterparts.[151]

It doesn't surprise us that research shows that having clarity about one's values and priorities significantly impacts a woman's sense of fulfillment and well-being. When women understand what truly matters to them, we're more likely to make decisions that align with our personal goals and needs. This not only boosts our confidence but also enhances our overall quality of life. To illustrate the power of clarity, take this story we heard from one young professional woman.

The Ditty Diaries: Paige's Story

For years, I was the friend who never missed a social event. Whether it was birthday parties, weekend trips, or spontaneous get-togethers, I was always there. I prided myself on being reliable and fun, but over time, I started to feel exhausted and drained. My calendar was always full, and I rarely had a moment to myself. My hobbies and personal interests were sidelined, and I felt like I was losing touch with who I really was.

One weekend, I decided to take a solo camping trip in the mountains to reflect on what truly mattered to me. Away from the constant invitations and social pressures, I spent my days hiking, meditating by the river, and enjoying the solitude of nature. During this time, I realized that my personal happiness, mental health, and time for self-reflection were my true priorities. I understood that while spending time with friends was important, it shouldn't come at the expense of my own well-being.

With this newfound clarity, I made a bold decision. I returned home and started to be more selective about the social events I attended. I explained to my friends that I needed to set some boundaries and prioritize my own needs. I began scheduling regular alone time, dedicating evenings to reading, painting, or simply relaxing at home.

*To my surprise, my friends were supportive and under-
standing. They respected my need for personal time and
even started to appreciate our time together more. With
my new balance, I felt more energized and fulfilled. I had
time to explore my passions, take care of my mental and
physical health, and still enjoy meaningful social interactions without feeling overwhelmed. My clarity about my
values had given me the confidence to make changes
that transformed my life for the better.*

Paige's story is a perfect example of The Clear Crystal dynamic,
which is:

The Clear Crystal

/ˈklir/ /ˈkristil/ *proper noun*
> One who truly knows her Essentials and can in-
> stinctively identify energizing tasks versus drain-
> ing ones. She makes intentional choices that align
> with her priorities, allowing her to confidently say
> "yes" or "no" with crystal-clear clarity.

What are the signs that you're a Clear Crystal? Our top five are:

1. **You Feel a Little Like the Energizer Bunny:** Your tasks and
   responsibilities leave you feeling motivated and fulfilled rather than drained and overwhelmed.

2. **Stress? What Stress?** You've traded in the constant feeling of
   being overwhelmed for a more Zen-like state, because you're
   not overloaded with unnecessary commitments.

3. **You Actually Enjoy Your Hobbies:** Instead of hobbies gathering dust, you're spending quality time doing what you love,
   be it knitting cat sweaters or perfecting your karaoke skills.

4. **Your Calendar Isn't a Disaster Movie:** You've got plenty of time for what matters, and your schedule doesn't look like a scene from a chaotic blockbuster.

5. **Drama-Free Zone:** Your life isn't a soap opera because you're too busy enjoying what matters to get caught up in unnecessary drama.

Diva Dynamic: The Self-Confident Sage

In her book *Becoming*, Michelle Obama—another diva by any measure—declared, "Am I good enough? Yes, I am."[152]

Research has shown that...

- Self-confidence has been shown as an important quality for effective leaders.[153]

- Identifying and focusing on strengths have been shown to increase self-confidence. When we recognize and focus on our strengths, we feel more authentic, engaged, and capable.[154]

- Perhaps contrary to popular belief, research suggests confidence is relational—something that you receive, give, and grow through others.[155]

Self-confidence is a game changer for a woman's fulfillment and well-being. Studies have long shown that when we believe in ourselves and recognize our worth, we're more likely to pursue opportunities that align with what matters most to us, thus enhancing our overall quality of life. With a healthy dose of self-confidence, we can more easily Ditch those pesky Ditties and embrace the Delights that truly light us up. To illustrate, consider this story.

The Ditty Diaries: Ophelia's Story

A few years ago, I found myself in a situation that tested my newfound self-confidence. As a young professional, I was eager to make a good impression and often found it hard to say "no" to extra work or social obligations. One day, my boss asked me to take on a major project that required working late nights and weekends. I knew this would severely impact my personal time and well-being.

In the past, I would have agreed without hesitation, fearing that saying "no" would make me seem uncommitted or incapable. But I had been working on building my self-confidence and understanding my worth. I realized that my skills and dedication were already proven, and that I didn't need to sacrifice my personal life to demonstrate my value.

Taking a deep breath, I decided to have an honest conversation with my boss. I explained that while I appreciated the opportunity, I had to decline the project due to my current workload and need for work-life balance. I suggested a few colleagues who might be a good fit for the project instead.

To my surprise, my boss was understanding and respected my decision. He appreciated my honesty and willingness to find an alternative solution. This experience reinforced my belief in the power of self-confidence. By saying "no" to something that didn't align with my priorities, I was able to maintain my well-being and focus on the tasks that truly mattered to me.

Ophelia's story is a great example of what The Self-Confident Sage sounds like. We define this Diva Dynamic as:

The Self-Confident Sage

/ˈself/ / ˈkänfəd(ə)nt/ /sage/ *proper noun*
> She knows her strengths and priorities, tackling challenges head-on. Her decisions are made with conviction, allowing her to embrace new opportunities and make courageous, confident choices.

We loved hearing Ophelia's story not only because we were happy for her, but because it strengthened our own self-confidence to say "no" to Ditties in our own lives. This feeling aligns with the research that suggests that confidence is not a fixed trait but something we can build, especially when we support and uplift each other. That's right. Real divas know that confidence is a collective sport. When we share our stories and support one another, we create a ripple effect that empowers us all. By building each other up, we cultivate a community where everyone feels strong enough to set boundaries and prioritize their true Essentials.

Because we love the notion of The Self-Confident Sage being contagious—in a good way—we want to share our top five ways that you can not only build your own confidence, but those of others around you. It's a beautiful, mutually reinforcing loop!

1. **Party for Progress:** Celebrate every milestone together—whether it's a promotion, a project completed, or a personal achievement. High-fives and cheers all around!

2. **Be a Confidence Coach:** Act as a mentor or find mentors who can provide guidance and encouragement. Sharing wisdom helps everyone navigate life's twists and turns with confidence.

3. **Ear to Hear:** Sometimes, just being there to listen and offer emotional support can make a huge difference. Knowing someone's got your back makes you braver.

4. **Adventure Buddies:** Encourage each other to try new things together, like a dance class or hiking trip. Shared adventures build confidence and create awesome memories.

5. **Challenge Champions:** Create fun challenges, like a book club or a fitness goal, and support each other in achieving them. Meeting goals together builds confidence and camaraderie.

Diva Dynamic: The Wondering Woman

Eleanor Roosevelt—another diva who inspired us in many ways—once shared:

> *"I think, at a child's birth, if a mother could ask a fairy godmother to endow it with the most useful gift, that gift would be curiosity."*[156]

It turns out that:

- When women are curious and take the time to thoroughly investigate their options, they feel more confident in their decisions.[157]

- Curiosity has been shown to help us cope with feelings of rejection and even anxiety.[158]

- Research suggests that curiosity acts as a social glue that strengthens our relationships.[159]

Being curious and embracing our inner "wondering" woman helps us unmask those sneaky, disguised Ditties. When we approach each request with a sense of curiosity, we can dig deeper and uncover whether it truly aligns with our values and desires. By asking thoughtful questions and exploring the motivations behind what's being asked, we ensure that we're not just saying "yes" out of habit or obligation. This playful curiosity also extends to us—are we responding out of habit or true desire? By getting curious about our own reactions, we can sift through the noise, Ditch the Ditties, and confidently embrace the opportunities that genuinely light us up.

Take this story as an example.

The Ditching Diaries: Zoë's Story

A while back, I found myself roped into organizing our neighborhood's annual garage sale. While it sounded like a fun community activity at first, the reality quickly set in: endless coordination, managing schedules, and dealing with everyone's leftover junk. It was turning into a major Ditty, draining my weekends and enthusiasm.

One Saturday morning, instead of just pushing through my growing to-do list, I decided to get curious. I started by chatting with a few neighbors, casually asking what they enjoyed most about past garage sales and what they wished could be different. During these conversations, I discovered something surprising: many neighbors didn't really care about the garage sale itself; they just wanted a chance to socialize and connect.

Armed with this new insight, I proposed a new idea to the neighborhood: Instead of a traditional garage sale, why not have a community swap meet with a potluck? Everyone loved the idea. It was less about selling and more about sharing and enjoying each other's company.

By simply being curious and asking the right questions, I was able to transform a tedious Ditty into a delightful event that brought the neighborhood together without all the hassle. Plus, it freed up my weekends, allowing me to enjoy the things I love. This experience taught me that a little curiosity can go a long way in making sure I'm spending my time on things that truly matter.

Curiosity is a powerful tool for Ditching Ditties. It helps us look beyond the surface to understand the true essence of requests and whether they align with our Essentials. By asking thoughtful questions, we can discern the motivations behind requests and unmask many of those dangerous Ditty Disguises.

Being curious about ourselves is also crucial for breaking free from habitual dynamics. By examining why we respond the way we do, we can uncover patterns that may not serve us. Are we saying "yes" out of a genuine desire or a conditioned reflex? This self-curiosity allows us to interrupt automatic responses and make intentional choices. It aligns our actions with our Essentials, rather than just going through the motions. By questioning our habits and understanding our behavior, we can transform our decision-making, Ditch unwanted Ditties, and embrace opportunities that truly matter. Self-curiosity is a critical key to living a more authentic and fulfilling life.

Much like Zoë, we strive to be The Wondering Woman every day—asking questions of ourselves and others, ensuring we are continually using our Essentials as a life compass. We define this Diva Dynamic as:

The Wondering Woman

/ˈwənd(ə)riNG/ /ˈwoŏmən/ *proper noun*
   One who embraces curiosity, eager to learn about herself and others. She asks insightful questions, seeking deeper understanding in all parts of life. Her curiosity leads to thoughtful, informed decisions, making her journey one of constant growth and wonder.

Just as clarity, self-confidence, and curiosity can each transform our lives and help us master the art of saying "no" and "yes" with confidence and grace, combining these three traits creates a powerful force. Enter the Ditching Diva—a woman who excels at prioritizing her Essentials and confidently shedding tasks and obligations that don't align with what matters to her—defined as:

The Ditty-Ditching Diva

/didē/ /diCHiNG/ /ˈdēvə/ *noun*
> One who confidently uses her Essentials to guide her decisions and enjoys the freedom of saying "no" to what doesn't align with them. Her clarity, self-confidence, and curiosity help her prioritize needs without sacrificing meaningful relation- ships. By focusing on what matters most, she ded- icates her time and energy to what truly brings joy and fulfillment.

Does this sound like you? We hope that after being armed with all the new tricks and tips we've explored throughout this book, you're beginning to more fully embrace your inner Ditty-Ditching Diva!

As you do this, we'd like to close by telling you: "And she lived happily ever after!" We haven't lied to you yet, and we're not go- ing to start now. There's one last Ditch we invite you to do with us:

Ditch the Illusion of Happily Ever After

As women, we're often sold the story that if we tick all the right boxes—be good, be nice, be smart, work tirelessly, strive for per- fection—we'll eventually stumble upon our elusive "happily ever after." We've been fed the fairy tale narrative that our "happy" awaits us just "after" the next milestone…

…after we choose the right college.

…after we graduate with honors.

… after we find the perfect place to live.

… after we land that first big job.

…after we land that second or 22nd big job.

…after we find the ideal partner.

…after we decide to become mothers, or not.

… after we buy the right clothes.

… after we climb the corporate ladder, or don't.

…after we shed those extra pounds.

… after we take that trip.

…after our kids graduate (or finally move out).

…after we volunteer for that role.

…after we help others.

…after we clean the house.

…after we make everyone around us happy.

…after…after…after…

It's as if there's a checklist of achievements we must complete, and only *after* that are we deemed worthy of happiness. But what happens after we magically check off all those boxes? Do we finally reach an end point where we can kick back and revel in our well-deserved happiness? Or do we find ourselves chasing yet another elusive "ever after," perpetually striving for some distant state of fulfillment? The relentless pursuit of an idealized future creates a cycle of constant striving and yearning. We find ourselves endlessly chasing an elusive destination, with the Ditty and Ditching Dynamics playing out like a recurring soundtrack in our lives.

Thus, as we reach the final pages of our journey together, it's essential to acknowledge that the quest for a "happily ever after" is a mirage that disappears upon closer inspection. Even armed with our newfound skills and insights, life will continue to throw Ditties our way. However, instead of viewing this reality as a setback, let's embrace it as an invitation—a call to adventure in ongoing Ditching that promises growth, resilience, and endless possibilities.

It's time we redefine "ever after" not as a distant end point but as the journey itself—a journey where fulfillment and joy are found not in reaching some predetermined objective but in embracing the messy, imperfect beauty of the present moment. Ditching Ditties isn't a destination—it's a lifelong adventure, an ongoing process of self-discovery and empowerment. It's about continuing to cultivate the courage to say "no" to what no longer serves us and the wisdom to say "yes" to what sparks joy and delight.

So, let's bid farewell to the promise of fairy tale endings and instead embrace the messy, beautiful reality of life—a journey filled with twists and turns, challenges and triumphs. Thus, our final wish for you is that you:

Live happily ever along.

We hope that you continue to navigate this wild and wonderful adventure of womanhood with grace, humor, and an irreverent spirit. We hope that you find delight in happily ever along the way, including…

>…along the way of navigating jobs that stress you out.

>…along the way of figuring out how to be a parent…or not.

>…along the way of discovering what matters to you, and then discovering it again and again as life evolves.

>…along the way of being there for loved ones who need you.

...along the way of finding the energy to keep going after your heart is broken.

...along the way of trying things that scare you.

...along the way of learning how to pivot when life throws you curve balls.

...along the way of showing up in the world in ways that are truly you.

So, here's to embracing the Ditty Ditching, the delightful discoveries, and everything in between, as we each continue to embrace the adventure of our "ever along." As such, this isn't "The End," but rather:

TO BE CONTINUED...

**Want to continue
the Ditty-Ditching conversation?**

**Visit us at www.ditchtheditty.com for more
stories, resources, and opportunities to connect with other Ditching Divas!**

Acknowledgements

We would like to express our deepest gratitude to those who have made our Ditty-Ditching journey possible.

First and foremost, to our families—thank you for your unwavering love, patience, and understanding as we took on this adventure. Your support has been our foundation, and your belief in us has fueled our courage, even on those days when we questioned ourselves and wondered how we would bring our Ditty-Ditching dream to life. From supporting our Ohio-Vermont trips to tolerating countless Zoom meetings and our never-ending "What do you think about this…?" requests, we know that this work could not have happened without you. To our spouses—Matt, Richard, and Beth—and to our children—Adam, Eliana, Elliot, Jackson, and Charlie—you are our anchors and our inspiration.

To our mothers and sisters, thank you for your constant encouragement, for always being there with a listening ear, and for your wisdom and guidance along the way. Your love and support have been a constant light, reminding us of the strength of women lifting each other up. We are profoundly grateful to all of you.

To our friends and colleagues, thank you for the countless conversations, your encouragement, and the inspiration you provided along the way. You helped us shape our ideas and kept us grounded, reminding us of the importance of this work. Special thanks to our earliest thinking partners and cheerleaders, including Maria Sirois, Sara Truebridge, Nadya Zhexembayeva, Mo McKenna, Betty Vandenbosch, Pru Sullivan, Jackie Stavros, Nicole Morris, Jessica Blackman, Mindy Kannard, Julie Rennecker, Mattison, Julia Zabell, Linda Wilkens, Sandy Wells, Frances Rucker-Bannister, Donna Sakony, Rebecca Coneglio, Dori Nelson-Hollis, Regina Loiko, and Jeny O'Connor-Neskey.

We are deeply grateful to our editor at Onion River Press, Rachel Carter, whose keen eyes, thoughtful suggestions, and tireless efforts helped bring clarity and strength to our words. Your dedication has been invaluable, and this book would not have been the same without you. And thank you to Rachel Fisher, Riley Earle, and the entire Onion River Press team for believing in this work and helping us make the book a reality.

A heartfelt thank you to Danielle Rini Uva and Katie Parland at Agnes Studio for their incredible work in bringing our brand and vision to life. Their creativity and dedication not only shaped the core of our visual identity but also designed the dynamic cover of this book, perfectly capturing its essence. We are grateful for their partnership and artistry.

To all those whose stories, wisdom, and insights have inspired us, and whom we quote within—thank you for sharing your light and knowledge. You have challenged us to think differently and have enriched our work with your perspectives.

And finally, to you, dear reader—thank you! Your curiosity, your quest for what truly matters, and your courage to Ditch the Ditties in your own life are exactly why we poured our hearts into this book. You're the reason we did this, and we can't wait to see where your Ditty-Ditching adventure leads you next!

With heartfelt thanks & loving irreverence,

Lindsey, Molly, and Miriam

References

1. Miller, Jo. "We Need to Talk About Office Housework." *Forbes*, 10 August 2020, https://www.forbes.com/sites/jomiller/2020/08/10/we-need-to-talk-about-office-housework.

2. Kay, Katty, and Claire Shipman. *The Confidence Code: The Science and Art of Self-Assurance—What Women Should Know.* HarperCollins, 2014.

3. Tulshyan, Ruchika, and Jodi-Ann Burey. "Stop Telling Women They Have Imposter Syndrome." *Harvard Business Review,* 11 February 2021, https://hbr.org/2021/02/stop-telling-women-they-have-imposter-syndrome.

4. Brown, Brené. *Atlas of the Heart: Mapping Meaningful Connection and the Language of Human Experience.* Random House Publishing Group, 2021.

5. Ehman, Karen. *When Making Others Happy Is Making You Miserable Bible Study Guide Plus Streaming Video: How to Break the Pattern of People Pleasing and Confidently Live Your Life.* HarperChristian Resources, 2022.

6. Castrillon, Caroline. "How Women Can Stop Apologizing and Take Their Power Back." *Forbes*, 14 July 2019,https://www.forbes.com/sites/carolinecastrillon/2019/07/14/how-women-can-stop-apologizing-and-take-their-power-back/

7. Ghodsee, Kristen R. "Women's Unpaid Labor is Worth $10,900,000,000,000." *The New York Times*, 5 March 2020, https://www.nytimes.com/interactive/2020/03/04/opinion/women-unpaid-labor.html.

8. Libby, Erin D. "Gender socialization: Implications for gender differences in self-concept among adolescents," 2007. *Master's Theses and Capstones.* https://scholars.unh.edu/thesis/45

9. Braiker, Harriet. *The Disease to Please: Curing the People-Pleasing Syndrome.* McGraw-Hill, 2001.

10. Frizzell, Nell. "A Timely Reminder: 'Invisible Labor' Is Still Work." *Vogue*, 19 December 2023, https://www.vogue.com/article/invisible-labor-is-still-work.

11. Deloitte Brandvoice. "Why Women Are Leaving the Workforce After the Pandemic—And How to Win Them Back." *Forbes*, 1 July 2021, https://www.forbes.com/sites/deloitte/2021/07/01/why-women-are-leaving-the-workforce-after-the-pandemic-and-how-to-win-them-back.

12. Fry, Richard. "During pandemic, some workforce disparities between men, women grew." *Pew Research Center*, 14 January 2022, https://www.pewresearch.org/short-reads/2022/01/14/some-gender-disparities-widened-in-the-u-s-workforce-during-the-pandemic.

13. Lipman, Joanne. "Essay | Return-to-Office Mandates Are a Disaster for Working Mothers." *Wall Street Journal*, 15 December 2023, https://www.wsj.com/lifestyle/careers/return-to-the-office-mandates-are-a-disaster-for-working-mothers-bf57a071.

14. Angelou, Maya. "Quote by Maya Angelou: 'Do the best you can until you know better. Then…'" Goodreads, https://www.goodreads.com/quotes/7273813-do-the-best-you-can-until-you-know-better-then.

15. Quinion, Michael. "Ditty bag." *World Wide Words*, 31 January 2015, https://www.worldwidewords.org/qa-dit2.html.

16. Guy, Olivia. "Gender Socialization: Examples, Agents & Impact." *Simply Psychology*, 13 February 2024, https://www.simplypsychology.org/gender-socialization.html.

17. Alu, Mary Ellen. "The Impacts of Gender Role Socialization on Health and Culture." *Lehigh University Research Review*, 5 April 2019, https://www2.lehigh.edu/news/the-impacts-of-gender-role-socialization-on-health-and-culture.

18. Miller, Claire Cain. "Why Unpaid Labor Is More Likely to Hurt Women's Mental Health Than Men's." *The New York Times*, 30 September 2022, https://www.nytimes.com/2022/09/30/upshot/women-mental-health-labor.html.

19. American Psychological Association. "Guidelines for Psychological Practice with Girls and Women." *American Psychological Association*, https://www.apa.org/practice/guidelines/girls-and-women.

20. Alu, Mary Ellen. "The Impacts of Gender Role Socialization on Health and Culture." *Lehigh University Research Review*, 5 April 2019, https://www2.lehigh.edu/news/the-impacts-of-gender-role-socialization-on-health-and-culture.

21. Wachowski, Lana and Wachowski, Lilly. *The Matrix,* 1999, Warner Bros.

22. Vidor, K., Fleming, V., Cukor, G., Thorpe, R., Taurog, N., & LeRoy, M. *The Wizard of Oz.* 1939. Metro-Goldwyn-Mayer (MGM).

23. Wachowski, Lana and Wachowski, Lilly. *The Matrix,* 1999, Warner Bros.

24. Vidor, K., Fleming, V., Cukor, G., Thorpe, R., Taurog, N., & LeRoy, M. *The Wizard of Oz.* 1939. Metro-Goldwyn-Mayer (MGM).

25. Ramis, Harold, *Groundhog Day*, 1993, Columbia Pictures.

26. Yang, John, and Harry Zahn. "As America's Population Ages, Women Shoulder the Burden as Primary Caregivers." NewsHour, 30 March 2024, https://www.pbs.org/newshour/show/as-americas-population-ages-women-shoulder-the-burden-as-primary-caregivers.

27. Superville, Denisa R. "Women in the K-12 Workforce, by the Numbers." *Education Week*, 8 March 2023, https://www.edweek.org/leadership/women-in-the-k-12-workforce-by-the-numbers/2023/03.

28. U.S. Bureau of Labor Statistics. "Employed persons by detailed occupation, sex, race, and Hispanic or Latino ethnicity." *Bureau of Labor Statistics*, 26 January 2024, https://www.bls.gov/cps/cpsaat11.htm.

29. Southwick, Ron. "Most registered nurses are women, but men get better pay, survey finds." *Chief Healthcare Executive*, 2 June 2022, https://www.chiefhealthcareexecutive.com/view/most-registered-nurses-are-women-but-men-get-better-pay-survey-finds.

30. Merriam Webster. "Opportunity Definition & Meaning." *Merriam-Webster*, https://www.merriam-webster.com/dictionary/opportunity.

31. Wachowski, Lana and Wachowski, Lilly. *The Matrix,* 1999, Warner Bros.

32. Vidor, K., Fleming, V., Cukor, G., Thorpe, R., Taurog, N., & LeRoy, M. *The Wizard of Oz*. 1939. Metro-Goldwyn-Mayer (MGM).

33. Opie, Iona, and Peter Opie. *The Oxford Dictionary of Nursery Rhymes*. Oxford University Press, 1997.

34. Tarrant, Shira. *Men and Feminism: Seal Studies*. Basic Books, 2009.

35. Kendall, Diana. *Sociology in Our Times*. Cengage Learning, 2017.

36. Gerwig, Greta, director. *Barbie*. 2023. Warner Bros. Pictures.

37. Li, Shirley. "Greta Gerwig's Lessons from Barbie Land." *The Atlantic*, 25 July 2023, https://www.theatlantic.com/culture/archive/2023/07/barbie-movie-greta-gerwig-interview/674817.

38. Lindsey, Linda. *Gender Roles: A Sociological Perspective*. New York: Taylor & Francis Group, 2015.

39. Celestino, Linda. "Why Is It So Hard for Women to Say No at Work?" *Fortune*, 12 July 2016, https://fortune.com/2016/07/12/career-advice-women.

40. UNICEF. "Girls Spend 160 Million More Hours Than Boys Doing Household Chores Everyday." *UNICEF*, 7 October 2016, https://www.unicef.org/turkiye/en/node/2311.

41. Saner, Emine. "'The Woman's To-Do List Is Relentless': How to Achieve an Equal Split of Household Chores." *The Guardian*, 15 August 2022, https://www.theguardian.com/money/2022/aug/15/how-to-achieve-an-equal-split-of-household-chores-kate-mangino.

42. Rakshit, Devrupa. "What Is "Office Housework" and Why Are Women Mostly In Charge of It?" *The Swaddle*, 9 June 2021, https://www.theswaddle.com/what-is-office-housework-and-why-are-women-mostly-in-charge-of-it.

43. Ravanera, Carmina. "Women More Often Volunteer for Tasks That Hinder Their Promotability." *Institute for Gender and the Economy*, March 2017, https://www.gendereconomy.org/women-more-often-volunteer-for-tasks-that-hinder-their-promotability.

44. Liesch, Kristen. "Who's Doing the Office Housework?" *Tidal Equality*, 30 January 2020, https://www.tidalequality.com/blog/whos-doing-the-office-housework.

45. Debuk. "Why women talk less—language: a feminist guide." *language: a feminist guide*, 23 May 2015, https://debuk.wordpress.com/2015/05/23/why-women-talk-less.

46. Debuk. "Why women talk less—language: a feminist guide."

47. Kinahan, Danielle. "Why Do We Have Such a Problem with the Way Women Speak?" *The Walrus*, 20 December 2018, https://thewalrus.ca/why-do-we-have-such-a-problem-with-the-way-women-speak.

48. Aznar, Ana, and Harriet R. Tenenbaum. "Gender and age differences in parent–child emotion talk." *British Journal of Developmental Psychology*, vol. 33, no. 1, 2015, pp. 148-155.

49. Briscoll, Victoria L. "Can an Angry Woman Get Ahead?: Status Conferral, Gender, and Expression of Emotion in the Workplace." Gender Action Portal, March 2008, https://gap.hks.harvard.edu/can-angry-woman-get-ahead-status-conferral-gender-and-expression-emotion-workplace.

50. Jacobson, Rae. "Why Girls Apologize Too Much." *Child Mind Institute*, 12 January 2024, https://childmind.org/article/why-girls-apologize-too-much.

51. Bleidorn, Wiebke, et al. "Age and Gender Differences in Self-Esteem—A Cross-Cultural Window." *Journal of Personality and Social Psychology*, vol. 111, no. 3, 2016, pp. 396-410. American Psychological Association, https://www.apa.org/pubs/journals/releases/psp-pspp0000078.pdf.

52. Allison, Catherine. "Nice Girls Should Be Seen and Not Heard." LinkedIn, 8 March 2017, https://www.linkedin.com/pulse/nice-girls-should-seen-heard-catherine-allison.

53. LeanIn.Org and McKinsey & Company Women in the Workplace Study. "Black women face more bias and get less support." *LeanIn.org*, September 2021, https://leanin.org/article/women-in-the-workplace-black-women.

54. Ross, Kendra J. "The Invisible Burden: Understanding the Emotional Labor of Black Women in the Workplace." LinkedIn, 28 November 2023, https://www.linkedin.com/pulse/invisible-burden-understanding-emotional-labor-black-women-ross-phd-ejdcc.

55. Tulshyan, Ruchika. "Women of Color Get Asked to Do More 'Office Housework.'" Here's How They Can Say No." *Harvard Business Review*, 6 April 2018, https://hbr.org/2018/04/women-of-color-get-asked-to-do-more-office-housework-heres-how-they-can-say-no.

56. Brownlee, Dana. "Dear Corporate America: Stop Tone Policing Black Women. We Have Every Right To Be Angry." *Forbes*, 23 November 2021, https://www.forbes.com/sites/danabrownlee/2021/11/23/dear-corporate-america-stop-tone-policing-black-women-we-have-every-right-to-be-angry.

57. Hunt, Meredith. "Women of Color in the Workplace: Navigating the Common Challenges." *Business 360 Blog*, 2022, https://business360.fortefoundation.org/women-of-color-in-the-workplace-navigating-the-common-challenges.

58. Royal, Cathy. "Quadrant Behavior Theory: Edging the Center." Handbook for Strategic HR: Best Practices in Organization Development from the OD Network, edited by John Vogelsang et al., AMACOM Division of American Management Association International, 2013, pp. 182-190.

59. Jerkins, Morgan. *This Will Be My Undoing: Living at the Intersection of Black, Female, and Feminist in (White) America.* HarperCollins, 2018.

60. Kendall, Mikki. *Hood Feminism: Notes from the Women That a Movement Forgot.* Penguin Publishing Group, 2021.

61. Parker, Kim, et al. "2. Americans see different expectations for men and women." *Pew Research Center*, 5 December 2017, https://www.pewresearch.org/social-trends/2017/12/05/americans-see-different-expectations-for-men-and-women.

62. YouGov. "People-Pleasing | YouGov Poll: June 18–21, 2022." *YouGov*, 19 August 2022, https://today.yougov.com/society/articles/43486-people-pleasing-yougov-poll-june-18-21-2022.

63. Yang, Kaite, and Joan S. Girgus. "Are Women More Likely Than Men Are to Care Excessively about Maintaining Positive Social Relationships? A Meta-Analytic Review of the Gender Difference in Sociotropy." *Stockton University*, Springer Science + Business Media, 2018, https://stockton.edu/social-behavioral-sciences/documents/yang1.pdf.

64. Goudreau, Jenna. "Why It's Hard for Women to Say 'No' at Work." *Business Insider,* 17 December 2014, https://www.businessinsider.com/why-hard-for-women-to-say-no-at-work-2014-12.

65. Oxford University Press. "People-pleaser." *Oxford English Dictionary*, 2005, https://www.oed.com/dictionary/people-pleaser_n?tl=true.

66. Guttman, Jennifer. "Beware: People-Pleasing Behaviors Can Backfire." *Psychology Today*, 2 August 2019, https://www.psychologytoday.com/ca/blog/sustainable-life-satisfaction/201908/beware-people-pleasing-behaviors-can-backfire.

67. Martin, Sharon, and Ivan Jevtic. "The Need to Please: The Psychology of People-Pleasing." *Psych Central*, 24 January 2020, https://www.livewellwithsharonmartin.com/psychology-of-people-pleasing.

68. Rakshit, Devrupa. "Why People-Pleasing Is a Common Human Instinct." *The Swaddle*, 6 November 2020, https://www.theswaddle.com/why-people-pleasing-is-a-common-human-instinct.

69. Sharpe, Gavin. "The Invisible Disease to Please." *Medium*, 6 October 2019, https://medium.com/invisible-illness/the-invisible-disease-to-please-bb63420e9bad.

70. Smyth, Teyhou. "Are Women Pressured into Unhealthy People-Pleasing?" *Thrive Global*, 20 July 2020, https://community.thriveglobal.com/are-women-pressured-into-unhealthy-people-pleasing.

71. Ward, Mary. "Women more likely to be perfectionists, anxious at work." *The Sydney Morning Herald*, 17 April 2018, https://www.smh.com.au/lifestyle/health-and-wellness/women-more-likely-to-be-perfectionistic-anxious-at-work-20180412-p4z971.html.

72. British Broadcasting Corporation. "Perfectionism hits working women." *News BBC*, 28 May 2009, http://news.bbc.co.uk/2/hi/health/8072739.stm.

73. British Broadcasting Corporation. "Perfectionism hits working women." *News BBC*, 28 May 2009, http://news.bbc.co.uk/2/hi/health/8072739.stm.

74. Moore, Scott, and Jon Lucas, directors. *Bad Moms.* 2016, Universal Pictures Home Entertainment.

75. Davis, Paula. "Let's Teach Girls to Be Brave, Not Perfect." *Forbes*, 8 March 2017, https://www.forbes.com/sites/pauladavislaack/2017/03/08/lets-teach-girls-to-be-brave-not-perfect.

76. Kay, Katty, and Claire Shipman. *The Confidence Code: The Science and Art of Self-Assurance---What Women Should Know.* HarperCollins, 2014.

77. Swider, Brian, et al. "The Pros and Cons of Perfectionism, According to Research." *Harvard Business Review*, 27 December 2018, https://hbr.org/2018/12/the-pros-and-cons-of-perfectionism-according-to-research.

78. Dweck, Carol S. *Mindset: The New Psychology of Success.* Ballantine Books, 2008.

79. Davis, Paula. "Let's Teach Girls To Be Brave, Not Perfect." *Forbes*, 8 March 2017, https://www.forbes.com/sites/pauladavislaack/2017/03/08/lets-teach-girls-to-be-brave-not-perfect.

80. Kay, Katty, and Claire Shipman. *The Confidence Code: The Science and Art of Self-Assurance—What Women Should Know.* HarperCollins, 2014.

81. Kay, Katty, and Claire Shipman. *The Confidence Code.*

82. Paulise, Luciana. "75% of Women Executives Experience Imposter Syndrome in the Workplace." *Forbes*, 8 March 2023, https://www.forbes.com/sites/lucianapaulise/2023/03/08/75-of-women-executives-experience-imposter-syndrome-in-the-workplace.

83. Angelou, Maya (n.d.). "Each time I write a book…" Goodreads. https://www.goodreads.com/quotes/220406-each-time-i-write-a-book-every-time-i-face.

84. Ball, Aimee Lee. "Women and the Negativity Receptor." *O, The Oprah Magazine*, August 2008, https://www.oprah.com/omagazine/why-women-have-low-self-esteem-how-to-feel-more-confident/all.

85. Baker, Darren T., and Juliet Bourke. "How Confidence Is Weaponized Against Women." *Harvard Business Review*, 20 October 2022, https://hbr.org/2022/10/how-confidence-is-weaponized-against-women.

86. Psychology Today. "Imposter Syndrome." *Psychology Today*, https://www.psychologytoday.com/us/basics/imposter-syndrome.

87. Anderson, L.V. "Feeling Like an Imposter Is Not a Syndrome." *Slate*, 12 April 2016, https://slate.com/business/2016/04/is-impostor-syndrome-real-and-does-it-affect-women-more-than-men.html.

88. Nance-Nash, Sheryl. "Why imposter syndrome hits women and women of colour harder." *BBC*, 27 July 2020, https://www.bbc.com/worklife/article/20200724-why-imposter-syndrome-hits-women-and-women-of-colour-harder.

89. Sandberg, Sheryl. *Lean In: Women, Work, and the Will to Lead.* Knopf, 2013.

90. Orr, Marissa. *Lean Out: The Truth about Women, Power, and the Workplace.* Harper Collins, 2019.

91. Plata, Mariana. "How to Spot Your Emotional Triggers." *Psychology Today*, 31 October 2018, https://www.psychologytoday.com/us/blog/the-gen-y-psy/201810/how-spot-your-emotional-triggers.

92. Lucas, George. *Star Wars Episode IV: A New Hope.* 1997, Lucasfilm.

93. Seppälä, Emma. "The Science of Intuition—and How to Tune into Your Own" *Time*, 23 April 2024, https://time.com/6837634/how-to-be-more-intuitive.

94. Spice Girls. "Wannabe." Song. Richard "Biff" Stannard & Matt Rowe, 1996.

95. Hasseldine, Rosjke. "Why Do Women Find It So Difficult to Put Themselves First?" *HuffPost*, 22 June 2015, https://www.huffpost.com/entry/why-do-women-find-it-so-d_b_7621976.

96. Hasseldine, Rosjke. "Why Do Women Find It So Difficult to Put Themselves First?" *HuffPost*, 22 June 2015, https://www.huffpost.com/entry/why-do-women-find-it-so-d_b_7621976.

97. Eyal, Maytal. "Self-Silencing Is Making Women Sick." *Time*, 3 October 2023, https://time.com/6319549/silencing-women-sick-essay.

98. Newport Institute. "Self-Silencing: The Mental Health Impact." *Newport Institute*, 26 October 2023, https://www.newportinstitute.com/resources/empowering-young-adults/self-silencing.

99. Hogenboom, Melissa. "The hidden load: How 'thinking of everything' holds mums back." *BBC*, 18 May 2021, https://www.bbc.com/worklife/article/20210518-the-hidden-load-how-thinking-of-everything-holds-mums-back.

100. Parker, Kim, et al. "Americans see different expectations for men and women." *Pew Research Center*, 5 December 2017, https://www.pewresearch.org/social-trends/2017/12/05/americans-see-different-expectations-for-men-and-women.

101. Thaves, Bob. Frank and Ernest. Cartoon. 1982. Goodreads, https://www.goodreads.com/quotes/192006-sure-he-was-great-but-don-t-forget-that-ginger-rogers.

102. Pleck, Joseph H. *The Myth of Masculinity.* MIT Press, 1981.

103. Heilman, Madeline. "Description and Prescription: How Gender Stereotypes Prevent Women's Ascent Up the Organizational Ladder." *The Journal of Social Issues*, vol. 21, no. Winter, 2002, pp. 657-674.

104. Braun, Stephen, et al. "Think manager—think male, think follower—think female: Gender bias in implicit followership theories." *Journal of Applied Social Psychology,* vol. 47, no. 7, 2017, pp. 377-388.

105. Brands, Raina. "'Think manager, think man' stops us seeing women as leaders." *The Guardian*, 15 July 2015, https://www.theguardian.com/women-in-leadership/2015/jul/15/think-manager-think-man-women-leaders-biase-workplace.

106. Argawal, Pragya. "Not Very Likeable: Here Is How Bias Is Affecting Women Leaders." *Forbes*, 23 October 2018, https://www.forbes.com/sites/pragyaagarwaleurope/2018/10/23/not-very-likeable-here-is-how-bias-is-affecting-women-leaders.

107. Maslow, A. H. "A Theory of Human Motivation." *Psychological Review*, vol. 50, no. 4, 1943, pp. 370-396.

108. Denning, Steve. "What Maslow Missed." *Forbes*, 29 March 2012, https://www.forbes.com/sites/stevedenning/2012/03/29/what-maslow-missed/?sh=4ebcac1d661b.

109. Khalil, Hafsa. "Marie Kondo is focusing on what's important—and that means letting the tidying slide." *CNN*, 30 January 2023, https://www.cnn.com/2023/01/30/entertainment/marie-kondo-stops-tidying-intl-scli/index.html.

110. Koncius, Jura. "Decluttering queen Marie Kondo turns her focus to creating inner calm." Washington Post, 26 January 2023, https://www.washingtonpost.com/home/2023/01/26/marie-kondo-kurashi-inner-calm.

111. Drucker, Peter F. *Managing for Results.* HarperCollins, 2006.

112. John, Elton. "Sorry Seems to Be the Hardest Word." Song. Gus Dudgeon, 1976.

113. Manning, Vivian. "How to stop saying 'I'm sorry' all the time—and what to say instead." *NBC News*, 5 October 2018, https://www.nbcnews.com/better/pop-culture/how-stop-saying-i-m-sorry-all-time-what-say-ncna917011.

114. Schumann, Karina, and Michael Ross. "Why Women Apologize More Than Men: Gender Differences in Thresholds for Perceiving Offensive Behavior." *Psychological Science*, vol. 21, no. 11, 2010, pp. 1649-1655.

115. Schumann, Karina, and Michael Ross. "Why Women Apologize More Than Men: Gender Differences in Thresholds for Perceiving Offensive Behavior." *Psychological Science*, vol. 21, no. 11, 2010, pp. 1649-1655.

116. Cauterucci, Christina. "New Chrome app helps women stop saying 'just' and 'sorry' in emails," *Slate*, 29 December 2015, https://slate.com/human-interest/2015/12/new-chrome-app-helps-women-stop-saying-just-and-sorry-in-emails.html.

117. Parker, Trey, et al. *South Park: Bigger, Longer & Uncut.* 1999, Paramount.

118. Engel, Beverly. "The Power of Apology." *Psychology Today*, 1 July 2002, https://www.psychologytoday.com/us/articles/200207/the-power-apology .

119. Jovanovic, Maja. *Hey Ladies, Stop Apologizing ... and Other Career Mistakes Women Make: New 2017-2018 Edition.* Rock's Mills Press, 2017.

120. Hinshaw, Stephen, and Rachel Kranz. *The Triple Bind: Saving Our Teenage Girls from Today's Pressures.* Random House Publishing Group, 2009.

121. Jacobson, Rae. "Why Girls Apologize Too Much." *Child Mind Institute*, 12 January 2024, https://childmind.org/article/why-girls-apologize-too-much.

122. Tavakoli, Nastaran, and Lois Wyse. "Perspective | Naomi Osaka apologizing for winning is the other tragedy of the U.S. Open." *The Washington Post*, 12 September 2018, https://www.thelily.com/naomi-osaka-apologizing-for-winning-is-the-other-tragedy-of-the-us-open.

123. Today Show. "TODAY Show." *Twitter*, 10 September, 2018, https://twitter.com/TODAYshow/status/1039127654820196352.

124. Castrillon, Caroline. "How Women Can Stop Apologizing and Take Their Power Back." *Forbes*, 14 July 2019, https://www.forbes.com/sites/carolinecastrillon/2019/07/14/how-women-can-stop-apologizing-and-take-their-power-back/?sh=739b22bb4ce6.

125. Nirvana. (1993). All apologies. On In utero. DGC Records.

126. McFaul, Ryan, director. "I'm Sorry." Inside Amy Schumer, created by Amy Schumer, season 3, episode 4, Comedy Central, 2015.

127. Gray, Emma, and Matt Sayles. "Amy Schumer Skewers a Culture That Makes Women Apologize All the Time." *HuffPost*, 14 May 2015, https://www.huffpost.com/entry/amy-schumer-im-sorry-not-sorry_n_7276504.

128. Simonson, Jordan, et al. "Socialized to Ruminate? Gender Role Mediates the Sex Difference in Rumination for Interpersonal Events." *Journal of Social and Clinical Psychology*, vol. 30, no. 9, 2011, pp. 937-959.

129. Lilly, Kieren, et al. "Thinking twice: examining gender differences in repetitive negative thinking across the adult lifespan." *Frontiers*, 8 November 2023, https://www.frontiersin.org/journals/psychology/articles/10.3389/fpsyg.2023.1239112/full#ref32.

130. Salk, Rachel H., et al. "Gender Differences in Depression in Representative National Samples: Meta-Analyses of Diagnoses and Symptoms." *Psychol. Bulletin*, vol. 143, no. 8, 2017, pp. 783-822.

131. Seuss, Dr. *How the Grinch Stole Christmas*. Random House, 1957.

132. American Psychological Association. "Someone to Complain with Isn't Necessarily a Good Thing, Especially for Teenage Girls." *American Psychological Association*, https://www.apa.org/news/press/releases/2007/07/co-rumination.

133. American Psychological Association. "Someone to Complain with Isn't Necessarily a Good Thing, Especially for Teenage Girls." *American Psychological Association*, https://www.apa.org/news/press/releases/2007/07/co-rumination.

134. Ehring, Thomas. "Thinking too much: rumination and psychopathology." *National Center for Biotechnology Information*, 9 September 2021, https://www.ncbi.nlm.nih.gov/pmc/articles/PMC8429319.

135. Schmitt, David P. "Are Men More Helpful, Altruistic, or Chivalrous Than Women?" *Psychology Today*, 10 March 2016, https://www.psychologytoday.com/us/blog/sexual-personalities/201603/are-men-more-helpful-altruistic-or-chivalrous-women.

136. Hathaway, Bill. "On first instinct, women are more altruistic than men." *YaleNews*, 25 February 2016, https://news.yale.edu/2016/02/25/first-instinct-women-are-more-altruistic-men.

137. University of Zurich. "The female brain reacts more strongly to prosocial behavior than the male brain, study finds." *ScienceDaily*, 9 October 2017, https://www.sciencedaily.com/releases/2017/10/171009123213.htm.

138. Ritvo, Eva. "The Neuroscience of Giving." *Psychology Today*, 24 April 2014, https://www.psychologytoday.com/us/blog/vitality/201404/the-neuroscience-giving.

139. University of Zurich. "The female brain reacts more strongly to prosocial behavior than the male brain, study finds." *Science Daily*, 9 October 2017. www.sciencedaily.com/releases/2017/10/171009123213.htm.

140. Lamia, Mary C., and Marilyn J. Krieger. *The White Knight Syndrome: Rescuing Yourself from Your Need to Rescue Others.* Echo Point Books and Media, 2015.

141. Cherry, Kendra. "How to Stop People-Pleasing." *Verywell Mind*, 19 May 2024, https://www.verywellmind.com/how-to-stop-being-a-people-pleaser-5184412.

142. Lamott, Anne. "'No' is a complete sentence."Goodreads, https://www.goodreads.com/quotes/24553-no-is-a-complete-sentence.

143. Reiner, Rob, director. This Is Spinal Tap. 1984, Embassy Home Entertainment.

144. Seuss, Dr. *Green Eggs and Ham.* Random House Children's Books, 1960.

145. Brown, Brené, and Rachel Antonik. "Clear Is Kind. Unclear Is Unkind." *Brené Brown*, 15 October 2018, https://brenebrown.com/articles/2018/10/15/clear-is-kind-unclear-is-unkind.

146. Palahniuk, Chuck. *Fight Club.* New York, W.W. Norton & Co., 2005.

147. O, The Oprah Magazine. "What Oprah Knows for Sure About Getting Unstuck." *Oprah.com*, September 2005, https://www.oprah.com/spirit/what-oprah-knows-for-sure-about-getting-unstuck.

148. Hakim, Ghenwa Al, et al. "Women's Empowerment as an Outcome of NGO Projects: Is the Current Approach Sustainable?" *Administrative Sciences*, vol. 12, no. 2, 2022. MDPI, https://www.mdpi.com/2076-3387/12/2/62.

149. Hakim, Ghenwa Al, et al. "Women's Empowerment as an Outcome of NGO Projects: Is the Current Approach Sustainable?" *Administrative Sciences*, vol. 12, no. 2, 2022. MDPI, https://www.mdpi.com/2076-3387/12/2/62.

150. Racioppi, Rosina L. "Clarity: An Often-Ignored Path to DEI." *Women Business Collaborative*, 27 March 2023, https://wbcollaborative.org/insights/clarity-an-often-ignored-path-to-dei/.

151. Glener, Doug. "The Extraordinary Benefits of Leadership Self-Awareness." *Blanchard*, 3 January 2023, https://resources.blanchard.com/blanchard-leaderchat/the-extraordinary-benefits-of-leadership-self-awareness.

152. Obama, Michelle. *Becoming.* Crown, 2018.

153. Axelrod, Ruth H. "(PDF) Leadership and Self-Confidence." *ResearchGate*, 14 August 2017, https://www.researchgate.net/publication/318029583_Leadership_and_Self-Confidence.